THE CYMRY OF '76;

OR,

WELSHMEN AND THEIR DESCENDANTS OF THE AMERICAN REVOLUTION.

AN ADDRESS:

WITH AN

APPENDIX,

CONTAINING

NOTES, SKETCHES, AND NOMENCLATURE OF THE

Cymbri;

BY ALEXANDER JONES, M.D.

AUTHOR OF "HISTORY OF THE ELECTRIC TELEGRAPH, &C."

TO WHICH IS ADDED

A LETTER ON EMINENT WELSHMEN. BY SAMUEL JENKINS, ESQ.

AND

A BRIEF SKETCH OF ST. DAVID'S BENEVOLENT SOCIETY.

SECOND EDITION.

CLEARFIELD

Second Edition
New York, 1855

Reprinted
Genealogical Publishing Company
Baltimore, 1968

Reprinted for
Clearfield Company, Inc., by
Genealogical Publishing Co., Inc.
Baltimore, Maryland
1985

Library of Congress Catalog Card Number 68-54869
International Standard Book Number 0-8063-0195-3

Made in the United States of America

CONTENTS.

THE CYMRY OF '76

OR,
WELSHMEN AND THEIR DESCENDANTS OF THE
AMERICAN REVOLUTION

PREFACE.

The plan of the following Address, with accompanying materials, was at first projected on a quite limited scale, and its subsequent execution imposed the necessity of close condensation; hence, little more could be done than to give the mere headings of the subjects discussed, forming to some extent, a sort of general key or text-book to Welsh History; and which others better learned, and with more leisure, may hereafter be enabled to trace out in full relief.

Other daily occupation of the writer interfered, more or less, with the reduction of the varied and rich materials at hand into that compactness of form and system which was desirable. Nevertheless, many of the facts and views submitted, we trust, will be found novel and interesting to the general reader; and especially, so far as they go to elucidate the Ethnology of the Cymbrian tribes of Europe. Much confusion and error have prevailed in relation to this subject, attributable, we believe, chiefly to the circumstance, that those in many instances who have written on the races of Europe, failed to make themselves acquainted with the Cymbrian or Welsh language, and its kindred dialects.

The part taken in the American Revolution by Welshmen and their descendants, cannot fail to interest the people of this country, and especially, those of Cambrian origin.

The distinction attained by the Welsh and their descendants in the elevated walks of Theology, Poetry, Government, Arts and Sciences, cannot prove otherwise than interesting to those of the Cymry race in every land.

A. J.

New York, 1855

THE following Address was delivered in the Welsh Congregational Church, in Eleventh Street, New York, at the request of the St. David's Benevolent Society, on the eve of St. David's day, the 28th February, 1855.—Wm. Miles, Esqr., President of the Society, in the chair. The Meeting was opened by prayer, by the Rev. Mr. Davies.

At the conclusion of the Address, the following Resolution was offered by Wm. B. Jones, Esq., the Corresponding Secretary of the Society, seconded by Robert Evans, Esq., and unanimously adopted:—

"*Resolved*, That the thanks of this Society and of those present be tendered to the Speaker, for his interesting and instructive Address, and that a copy be requested for publication."

The request was at once made by the President, and acceded to by the Speaker. The Meeting was then dismissed by the Rev. Mr. Griffith, Pastor of the church.

ADDRESS.

"Loud Fame hath told their gallant deeds."

LADIES AND GENTLEMEN:—

I have chosen for the subject of my Address, this evening, THE CYMRY OF '76, or the Welshmen and their descendants of the American Revolution.

Would that some one not so humble as myself—some one better learned in the history and glorious deeds of the Cymry or Cambrian race, filled my place on the present occasion—one who had the knowledge, the zeal, and the eloquence, to exhibit to you all the leading traits in the history of one of the most remarkable races known in the family of nations—one who could tell you of a people, who have had a country and a language on the island of Britain, for twenty-four hundred years, which they maintained in unconquered and unconquerable possession, against all invaders*.—Who could tell you of a people who, starting west from the *Crimea*, the present Golgotha of the European war of civilization, against Tartarian barbarism, and trace its exodus west, through parts of Germany and northern Italy to a final home in Gaul and Britain—whose march to this promised land was marked by bloody conflicts with warlike nations, that sought to enslave them—among whom, the longest and most powerful enemy were the Romans; and against whose assumption of universal dominion, they contended as Cimbri, Kimri, or Cymry, in every position they occupied

* See Appendix, *Note* 1.

in Europe.—Who could relate to you the deeds of nearly 1,300 years, in British Cambria, against Roman, Saxon and Norman invaders; maintaining their country, laws, and language, to the last; the latter justly said to be the most extraordinary monument of antiquity extant*.—Who could point out to you the position of Wales, with her tall mountains and vast remains of British forts and castles, that everywhere mark the struggle of a brave people in defence of civil and religious liberty, for so many centuries—resembling the crumbling ruins of an immense Sebastopol; and tell you, that when civil and religious despotism deluged the rest of the world, in the home of the Briton, as if in a citadel appointed by God, was preserved the seed of civil and religious liberty. Cambria was ever the refuge of those who were persecuted for conscience' sake. I would that one stood before you, who could point out to you, in their true colors, the patriotic deeds of the Cymry and their descendants—not only in Wales but in both hemispheres—where their blood has been so freely poured out in defence of freedom. The soil of Europe and of America has received the ashes of those slain in defence of liberty; and the bravery of the 23d Royal Welsh Fusileers, at the battle of the Alma—where a majority of its officers and over one-half of the regiment fell, killed or wounded, in storming the strongest battery of cannon in the Russian lines—proved that the heroic fire of the ancient Briton still burned with undiminished brightness in the bosoms of the modern *Cymry*. I cannot pretend to do this; but, however obscure my position and unworthy I may be of the task, the fulness of my heart impels me to say something, in commemoration of the glorious deeds of the Cymry, and their descendants on the American continent, in behalf of the civil and religious liberty we now enjoy.

In all ages and throughout the entire pilgrimage of the race, its sentiment has been in favor of the liberty of the person and the freedom of the soul.

We find the substance of these principles embodied in the ancient Cambrian or British Laws, which date back to an immemorial period. The spirit of these laws inculcated truth

* See Appendix, *Note* 2.

honesty, justice, mercy, and liberty. Their sacred regard for truth secured freedom of conscience in religious belief. The motto of the Cymry has ever been—

"Y Gwir yn erbyn y Byd."
"Truth against the world."

It was this sentiment which animated John Rogers, who was of a Welsh family. When he was burnt at the stake in Smithfield, he might have exclaimed: "I die for the truth—the truth of God—against all the powers of earth and darkness." It was this which animated Sir J. Oldcastle, Baron Cobham—a man of Welsh family—when he expired on a gibbet. It was this sentiment which caused 4,000 Protestants or Huguenots to leave Brittany in France, at the revocation of the edict of Nantz, and to seek homes on distant lands; leaving behind a soil enriched by the blood of martyrs to the truth.* It has been this sentiment, traditionally handed down from sire to son, which, like the polar star, has guided the Cymry through past ages and animated their bosoms in every contest for freedom.

While nearly every country of Europe was desecrated by religious martyrdom, no smoke from the burning victims to bigotry, or groans from bloody gibbets, for conscience' sake, ever rose in the pure air of Wales. No Druid perished at the hand of the early Christian; or the latter at the hand of the former. Truth was sacred to all.

If we wish to trace the origin of the principles of the English Common Laws and of Magna Charter, as well as those proclaimed in the American Declaration of Independence, we must go back to the laws of the Ancient Britons; which were compiled by the great Cambrian law-giver, known as Dyfnwal Moelmud, and were said by some persons to have existed 400 years before the birth of Christ.† No system of laws can be complete without it embraces their principles. Blackstone states that the Common Laws of England existed on the Island from time immemorial; and hence, anterior to the Roman or Saxon invasion. They guaranteed equality of civil and religious rights and secured the pursuit of life, liberty, and happiness.

* See History of the French Protestant Refugees, by H. Charles Wiess.
† See Appendix, *Note* 3.

We have no time to give even a brief outline of these remarkable laws. They are couched in curious phrases, yet they are worthy of being studied by all jurists in search of the origin of laws.

They secured trial by jury, and recognised the principles of government in substance, as now divided into *Executive*, *Judicial*, and *Legislative* departments; which is nothing more than an ancient British Triad modernized.

It was these laws which the learned Welsh Bishop, Asser Manevensis, (a title or bardic *surname*,) translated into Latin for Alfred the Great, and which he again translated into Saxon, and had them extended over all the Heptarchies; and hence, from being made common over the Saxon part of the island, they came to be called the Common Laws of England. The University of Oxford was founded by Alfred, under the advice and assistance of Asser Manevensis; and four of its first professors were Britons.

When the Saxons first landed in England, the Britons had been in possession of Christianity from 400 to 500 years; it having been introduced, beyond all controversy, early in the first and not later than in about the middle of the second century.*

It was the love of civil and religious liberty which animated the Cymry in their battles against the Romans for 400 years. It was the same principle which caused them to war against the Saxons for 600 years; their bloodiest contest having been excited in opposition to the attempted secular usurpation of Rome exercised, through the first Saxon converts, in about the 6th century.† It was the same spirit which nerved them to war against the rapacious and bigoted Normans, for about 200 years, or until the year 1283.

It was in this year that Edward the First held his Parliament at Rhuddlan Castle, North Wales; and guaranteed, to a people he could not conquer, the continuance of their ancient laws, usages and municipal government; while they obtained a native representative in the royal family, in the person of the prince of Wales, giving only in return an outward allegiance

* See Thackeray's History of the Introduction of Christianity into Britain. Vol. 1. † See Appendix, *Note* 4.

to the crown.* They were never united to England under the same laws until the reign of the Tudors, of Welsh descent, on the male or Tudor side of the House; or until about the middle of the 16th century, in the reign of Henry Tudor the Eighth, and after that monarch had overthrown the authority of the Pope in England, which Henry Tudor the Seventh had so vigorously commenced, and which grand reform, Elizabeth Tudor so gloriously completed in her long and brilliant reign—surrounded as she was by a galaxy of dazzling intellects in the persons of Shakspeare, Bacon, Raleigh, Spenser, and others unequalled, if not, unsurpassed in the annals of civilization.†

Going back to the days of William the Norman, we find that he brought over with him a powerful Roman priesthood, who attempted to crush out the Common Laws of England, and to establish on their ruin the centralizing code of Justinian, which was more favorable to their extending and retaining secular power.

They had enthralled the continent under their centralizing despotism,—which is endured and felt, to some extent, even to the present day. They drove the Common Law studies from the universities of Oxford and Cambridge, and endeavored to expel them from the realm. The people, however, were attached to their ancient common laws; and many of the judges and lawyers sided with them. Hence arose the Common Law schools or colleges of London, known as the Inner Temple, Gray's Inn, Lincoln's Inn Fields, etc., which soon numbered over 1,000 students. The Court of Common Pleas becoming fixed in London, gave them permanent strength. They sustained the Common Laws,—the foundation of all modern liberty—which triumphed over the Justinian code, and which shone forth in all their glory in the reign of the Tudors.

It is the spirit of these laws which has at all times animated the Cambrian race. They inspired Cromwell and Milton, of Cambrian blood, when they struck for liberty and the commonwealth. They animated the brave men of Wales, when they aided to dethrone king Richard the Third; and, at a later period, the papal king James the Second. They inspired

* See Appendix. † Idem.

Roger Williams himself—born in Wales, in 1599, and who was a relative of the Protector—and was the first to establish a democracy on this continent, based upon the principles of civil and religious liberty, at Providence plantations. He proclaimed that toleration of the conscience was of God and not of man, and that the latter had no power to grant what he could not withhold. In 1636, just 139 years before our Declaration of Independence, we find that this humble Cambrian and Minister of God, taught and established its essential truths, in the small colony he had founded. The same spirit of laws, good-will, and love to man, animated William Penn, another great and good man of the Cambrian race having been connected on his father's side to the Tudors, and said to have been distantly related to the royal House of the Tudors—when he founded the noble State of Pennsylvania;—principles, which won friends among the wildest savages, and drew them to him as affectionate children to a parent. It was the spirit of these laws—exemplified in the peaceful and happy governments of Roger Williams and William Penn—which contributed to pave the way for our freedom, and animated the sages and soldiers of the American Revolution. They brought with them patriotism kindled at the altars of ancient British freedom, amidst the venerated hills and mountains of Cambria. They brought with them a courage and a faith, inspired at the graves of their fathers, who had fallen, while fighting, through twelve centuries, in defence of home and liberty.—

> "Rest, ye brave dead! 'midst the hills of your sires,
> Oh! who would not slumber when freedom expires?"

We shall proceed to speak of the Cymry and their descendants of the American Revolution. We shall lay before you their services in connexion with one of the most important events in the history of man, and which must forever challenge the attention of the historian. To have performed any part in the accomplishment of such a revolution, however humble, must confer unfading honor and imperishable fame. In that memorable contest many noble patriots were supplied by other countries of Europe—from France, Germany, Poland, England,

Ireland, and Scotland—whose services have received deserved gratitude and lasting eulogy.

We, this evening, on the eve of Cambria's national anniversary, propose to present to the public the claims of the Welsh people to their share of the honor gained by their participation in the same great contest.

The Cymry, as a race, have claims to share in the annual celebration of the event, while the liberty it has secured remains. And its people can appropriately dwell upon the character and deeds of those of *their race* who distinguished themselves during our long and severe struggle.

Among the noble band who signed the Declaration of Independence were seventeen men of Cambrian birth or origin. These we shall briefly enumerate as follows.

First and foremost was THOMAS JEFFERSON. His ancestors came from the foot of Mount Snowden, in Wales, to the colony of Virginia. He always boasted of his Ancient British blood. No man ever lived who was more strongly endued with the principles of civil and religious liberty. His motto was: "*Rebellion to Tyrants, is obedience to God.*" He also contended that error should be left free to be combatted by reason. He caused the first aphorism to be engraved on his seal. To attempt any sketch of his life and works, would fill volumes. His history, for a long period, was the history of his country. We can only briefly allude to a few of his prominent acts.

First. To the authorship of that undying instrument,—the Declaration of our Independence; the principles of which proclaimed freedom to down-trodden man, in all parts of the world, and told him of his inalienable rights to political, civil, and religious equality—an instrument looked up to by enslaved nations, as the unfading star of hope which is to guide them to the immortal temple of freedom.

It was a great and solemn event when the Declaration of Independence was adopted. We can imagine the solemn silence of that august body, on the fourth of July, 1776, when waiting for the committee which was charged to report it to Congress. We can see the streets crowded by a vast mass of anxious people, who were waiting in breathless anxiety to hear the result. We can see the gray-haired bell-ringer, as he sat on the belfry, with string in hand, ready to peal forth its joyful sounds and proclaim—

"Liberty, throughout the land, unto all the inhabitants thereof."

There sat John Hancock, the president of the convention. There were seen Robert Morris, Benj. Franklin, and other noble spirits, awaiting the report in calm dignity. We can imagine the death-like stillness which prevailed, when Benjamin Harrison, its chairman, accompanied by Jefferson and others, entered the hall. We can hear the president demanding to know if they are ready to report; when a responsive "Yes" is the reply; and the secretary proceed to read it in a strong and solemn voice. The president then demands a vote, saying: "All in favor of the report say '*Aye*'." As the names are called, an unanimous and solemn '*Aye*' comes forth from each and all those brave men. The president rises, and announces the Declaration of Independence carried unanimously, —when a loud and merry peal is sent forth from the bell above, while the people in the streets burst forth in shouts of frantic joy.

At that time tyranny covered the nations of the earth as "darkness upon the face of the deep." The governments of Europe, were steeped in corrupt despotism, nursed on the continent by a corrupt church. Austria slept in the arms of despotic rule. Spain and Italy governed through the Inquisition and the gibbet. And even in France, the nobility were living in besotted licentiousness and bigotry. The events of that auspicious day severed the American colonies from the crown of Spain. They destroyed the rotten boroughs of England, and gave Catholic Emancipation to Ireland. They hurled despots from power on the continent, and reconstructed governments on liberal principles. They gave a vast inter-oceanic continent to freedom, and erected the principles of civil and religious liberty on the rock of ages.

Second. To Thomas Jefferson is due the abolition of all connexion between church and state.

Third. The abolition in Virginia of all laws in favor of the rights of primogeniture.

Fourth. The restrictions imposed upon the Constitution,

for the better security of State rights, by having adopted the following clause :—

"The powers not delegated to the United States by the Constitution, nor prohibited by it to the States, are reserved to the States respectively ; or to the people."

Without his services, the Revolutionary war would have been more or less bootless ; and a government would have been erected essentially centralized and aristocratic in its principal features. He was not afraid to trust the people, provided proper and free education were imparted to them. His whole life was devoted to the best interest of his country. As President he administrated the government on strictly democratic principles, which have successfully guided it to the highest rank among the nations of the earth. Under the shield of its banner the oppressed of all nations find freedom and a home. It was during his administration that we acquired Louisiana, and planted our flag on the Gulf of Mexico, and on the shores of the Pacific.—

Lewis, who accompanied Clark to the Columbia river, was of a Welsh family. In their long and perilous journey, they lost but one man, William Floyd, of a Welsh family, and who was buried on top of a mound west of the Missouri,—called, to this day, *Floyd's Mound.*—

This great man's interest in the growth and prosperity of his country remained with him to the last, and its triumph in peace and in war never ceased to animate his bosom.

Eighty-four winters had passed over his head. 'He had fought the good fight.' He was now about to 'finish his course.' He had corresponded with another man of the Cambrian race —John Adams—to the close of life. They had been widely separated in their views as statesmen and, no doubt, honestly differed ; yet, they remained, with a brief interruption, warm personal friends. We know of no instance where men so widely differed regarding public measures, yet, so nobly and fraternally clung to each other. Early brothers in patriotism, they bequeathed to us an example of union above party strife, which we may do well to remember and emulate. Again, history supplies no coincidence like that which marked their decease on the same day, and on the 4th of July, 1826—a day which both had so largely contributed to render immortal. The sun that rose on that day—just fifty years after the Declaration of Independence, 'midst the roar of cannon and the rejoicings of a free people—set on the last existence of those great patriots; and the sage of Monticello was no more. If we visit his last home, we shall see, on a plain marble slab, the following inscription:—

"HERE LIES THOMAS JEFFERSON,
Author of the Declaration of Independence; of the Statute of Virginia for Religious Freedom; and Father of the University of Virginia."

BENJAMIN HARRISON, of Virginia, was chairman of the committee which reported the Declaration of Independence. His ancestors came from Wales to Virginia. He filled various public offices in his native State, including that of Governor. He retired from public life in 1785, and died on his farm in 1790. He was, as is well known, father of the late Wm. Henry Harrison, President of the United States, and who also served in the American Revolution.

Following the list of Signers of the Declaration of Independence, of Welsh birth or descent, we must commence with New England; which, from having received a large accession from the followers of Cromwell, after the Restoration, has always contained a large element of Welsh blood. Among many other men of Welsh origin or descent, known in her annals, may be mentioned Yale, the founder of Yale college, and Jonathan Edwards, one of her most learned Divines, and also Daniel Webster who, it is said, was descended from the Welsh, on his mother's side. Prior to the Revolution, New England, Pennsylvania, Delaware, Maryland, and Virginia received a large number of emigrants from Wales, many of whom and their descendants bore distinguished parts in the war of the American Revolution.

Among the Signers of the Declaration of Independence, of Welsh origin, we have two names, Samuel and John Adams, whose brilliant and patriotic services in the cause of the Revolution are so well and so widely known. Samuel Adams, the stirring orator and bold patriot of his time, was born in Boston, in 1722, and was educated for the ministry at Harvard College;

but he threw aside orders for politics, and the British government set a price upon his head. He served faithfully in the Continental Congress and afterwards assisted in framing the Constitution of his native State. He died on the 12th of October, 1803, aged 81 years. John Adams was born at Quincy, in Massachussetts, in 1735. He bore an active and brilliant part in the American Revolution, and signed the Declaration of Independence with the former. He died on the 4th of July, 1826, aged 91; having served as President and Vice President of the United States.

Rhode Island sent Stephen Hopkins to the convention, who came of a Welsh family. He was born in Providence, and was a self-taught man. He wrote and acted against the unjust political course of England, long before the Revolution, and after having filled important offices in his State, became a member of the first Continental Congress, and signed the Declaration of Independence. He died in July, 1785.

Connecticut supplied Wm. Williams, who belonged to a Welsh family, and graduated at Harvard College, in 1751, at 20 years of age. He studied Law, but afterwards changed to the profession of Arms, and was aid to his brother who fell at Fort George in 1755. He signed the Declaration of Independence in 1776, and died in 1811, aged 81 years.

New York sent four delegates to the Continental Congress, in 1776. Three of the number who pledged this great State and their own lives and fortunes to freedom and Independence, were Welshmen by birth or origin.

One was William Floyd, who was born on Long Island, in 1734. He was an early patriot, and quite wealthy; was in the first Continental Congress, in 1774, and signed the Declaration of Independence, in 1776. He was engaged in public life during the war, suffered great loss of property at the the hands of the English, and died in 1821, in his 87th year.

The second was Francis Lewis, who was born in the southern part of Wales, in 1713. He was partly educated in Scotland and at Westminster, London. He entered upon a mercantile life in London, from whence he came to New York and conducted business for English merchants. He was taken prisoner in the French war and carried to France; afterwards returned to New York, took an active part on the patriot side, and signed the Declaration of Independence as a delegate from New York. He owned property on Long Island, which was destroyed by the English, and died in 1803, aged 90 years. .

The third was Lewis Morris, who was born of a Welsh family, in 1726. He graduated at Yale college, in 1746, and then settled at the farm of his father, now known as Morrisania, in Westchester county. He took sides with the patriots, and was sent from New York to the Continental Congress in 1775, and served till 1777: having, in the mean time, signed the Declaration of Independence. He lost a large amount of property by the war, and died in 1798, aged 72.

We thus find that three, out of the four,—Signers, for what has since become the Empire State,—were of the Cambrian race. The fourth was Mr. Livingston, who was of Scotch descent, though his family came from Holland.

We come next to Pennsylvania, which was represented in the convention, among other Cymry, by Robert Morris, who was born in 1733. He came to this country when a child, and was educated in Philadelphia. He served an apprenticeship with a merchant, afterwards commenced business for himself, was remarkable for energy and integrity of character, and won the confidence of the community. He was elected a member of the Continental Congress, in 1776, and was considered the ablest financier in the country. For a long time, his individual credit was superior to that of Congress itself. He lost an immense fortune in the cause, and died in comparative poverty in 1806, aged 73 years.

Francis Hopkinson was descended from a Welsh family, and was a member of the Continental Congress, from New Jersey. He was born in Philadelphia, in 1737, became distinguished as a lawyer, and was noted as a wit and poet. He wrote several pamphlets in favor of the patriot cause, and was the author of *Hail Columbia,* our national air, and also wrote the *Battle of the Keggs.* He signed the Declaration of Independence, and afterwards became eminent as a judge in Pennsylvania. He died in May, 1791, in his 53d year of age

From his name, George Clymer was probably of Welsh

family descent; deriving his name, from the Welsh word Clymwr,—one that ties or makes a knot.

John Morton, of Pennsylvania, was a native of Delaware, and was descended from a Welsh family, on his mother's side; his father having been of Swedish descent. He was on the committee which reported the articles of confederation.

John Penn was of Welsh family, but born in Virginia. He studied law with Mr. Pendleton and afterwards settled in North Carolina; from whence he was sent to the Continental Congress, and signed the Declaration of Independence.

Arthur Middleton was of Welsh origin, and was born in South Carolina, in 1743. He graduated at the university of Cambridge, England, and returned to America in 1773. He was a delegate from South Carolina, and signed the Declaration of Independence. He was in Charleston when it surrendered to the British, and was taken prisoner. A large portion of a great fortune was sacrificed during the Revolution. He died in January, 1789, aged 44 years.

Button Gwinnett was a native of Wales, and a delegate from Georgia to the Continental Congress. He was born in 1732. He was well educated, and entered into mercantile pursuits in Charleston, from whence he removed to Georgia, where he had purchased a large tract of land. He signed the Declaration of Independence, and afterwards assisted in framing the State Constitution of Georgia, and was President of the State—an office, at that time, equivalent to Governor. He fell, at the age of 46, in a duel which he fought with General McIntosh, of that State.

Among the Signers from Virginia, besides Thomas Jefferson and Benj. Harrison, was Richard Henry Lee, who was also from a Welsh family. He was born in Westmoreland Co., Virginia, in 1732, and was educated in England, and soon after his return, in 1757, he was elected a member of the House of Burgesses. He was elected to the Continental Congress, in 1774; and in July, 1776, he had the HONOR TO OFFER THE RESOLUTION DECLARING THE COLONIES FREE AND INDEPENDENT. He was an active and influential member of Congress, during the greater part of the war, and was appointed U. States Senator, under the Constitution; which office he filled with great ability. He died June 19, 1794, in the 62nd year of his age.

FRANCIS HENRY LIGHTFOOT LEE was also a Signer from Virginia, and of Welsh origin. He was born in Virginia, on the 10th of Sept., 1734. He was educated at home, and from 1765 to 1775, served his State as a member of the House of Burgesses. He afterwards became a delegate to the Continental Congress, and signed the Declaration of Independence. He died in April, 1797, in his 61st year of age.

There have been five Presidents of the United States, who were said, on good historical grounds, to have been of Welsh descent: three of whom bore part, as soldiers, in the Revolutionary army. They were Thomas Jefferson, James Madison, James Monroe, and William Henry Harrison. To this list if we add, which we may do on what is said to be good authority, the names of John and John Quincy Adams, it would make seven executive officers of the United States, of Welsh descent.

The most distinguished jurist this country has ever produced, and who is known as the "American Mansfield," was the grandson of a native of Wales, who emigrated to Virginia —we allude to the late Chief Justice JOHN MARSHALL.* His father and himself were both in the field, as commissioned officers, under Washington, and were at the battles of Trenton, Princeton, Brandywine, Germantown, and Monmouth; and in winter quarters, at Valley Forge. And—as if the office belonged to the Cymry,—we understand, from his biography, that the present Chief Justice of the United States, Roger B. Taney, has descended from a Welsh family, of the northern part of Wales.†

We thus see that the first man who moved the Resolution in favor of Independence—the author of the Declaration of Independence, and the chairman of the committee who reported it, were of the Cambrian race; while another Cymro‡—Gouverneur Morris—wrote out the first connected draft of the American Constitution. And a noble Cymro,—John Marshall; as Chief

* See the "Lives of the Chief Justices of the United States," by George Van Santvoord. Scribner. New York, 1854. † Idem.

‡ In the Welsh language *Cymry* (pronounced *Kumre*) is plural, and *Cymro* singular.

Justice of the Union,—was the first who expounded and established its principles on the immutable bases of the Constitution and of the laws enacted under it; aided by the ideas of impartial equity and justice.

Our next purpose will be to give some account of those Cymry and their descendants, who fought and bled on the field of battle, in our Revolutionary struggle.

> "Warriors I saw who led the fray,
> Stern desolation strewed their way,
> Aloft the glittering blades they bore,
> Their garments hung with clotted gore,
> The furious thrust, the clanging shield,
> Confound the long disputed field."

Rome and Greece, in their purest and brightest days, produced no patriots more heroically devoted to liberty than the Cymry of the American Revolution. In their list of heroes may be found the following names:—

GENERALS.

1. Anthony Wayne,	8. Daniel Morgan,
2. Isaac Shelby,	9. John Cadwallader,
3. Morgan Lewis,	10. Andrew Lewis,
4. William R. Davie,	11. Otho H. Williams,
5. Edward Stephens,	12. John Thomas,
6. Charles Lee,	13. Jos. Williams,
7. Richard Winn,	14. James Reese.

COLONELS.

1. David Humphreys,	5. Henry Lee,
2. Lambert Cadwallader,	6. Thomas Marshall,
3. Richard Howell,	7. James Williams, killed at Benington, under Stark.
4. Ethan Allen.	

Dr. John Morgan, who was Surgeon-in-chief of the American army and one of the founders of the Philadelphia Medical School, the first institution of the kind established in America, was of a Welsh family.

Among the Captains of the Revolution was John Marshall,

the late Chief Justice; Rogers, who was with George Rogers Clark, in the conquest of Illinois; Anthony Morris, of Philadelphia, who fell at the battle of Princeton; Isaac Davis and Capt. Davis, who fell at the battle of Concord; Lieut. Shelby, who served in the expedition to the Scioto, in 1774.

Among the Divines of that period of the war were:—The Revs. David Jones, Samuel Davie, David Williams.

Among the framers of the American Constitution were:— Gouverneur Morris, William Few, James Madison, and others.*

In the Navy were:—Commodore Hopkins, of Rhode Island, and others.

We thus see, that there were 14 Generals, 7 Colonels, and a number of subordinate officers, of the Cambrian race and name engaged in the Revolution.

The history of their heroic deeds would fill volumes.

All we can do, on the present occasion, will be to notice a few of the most prominent among them.

We commence with General Wayne who, from his daring acts of courage, was called "*Mad Anthony.*" He was a Cymro by descent, on both his father's and his mother's side; the latter bore the name of Giddings or Gethings, pronounced in Welsh Gething. He was born in Chester County, Pennsylvania, in 1745, and was educated in Philadelphia and, like Washington, assumed the profession of a surveyor. In 1773, he entered the General Assembly of the State; but, soon after, relinquished his post and entered the field, as a soldier, in 1775. He received the appointment of Colonel, and went with General Thomas to Canada. At the close of the campaign he was appointed brigadier-general. He was with Washington at the hard-fought battles of Brandywine, Germantown, and Monmouth, in all of which he was distinguished for his valor.

One of the bravest exploits of the Revolutionary war was his capture, by storm, of Stony Point, on the Hudson river; which filled the country with joy and admiration. His watchword, on that occasion, borrowed from the enemy, was "the fort is our own." He announced his victory in the following laconic letter to the commander-in-chief:

* At a later period were Commodores Rogers, Perry, Jacob Jones, and Ap Catesby Jones.

"STONY POINT, 16*th July*, 1779.
2 o'clock, A. M.

DEAR GENERAL:—

THE Fort and Garrison, with Col. Johnson, are ours. Our officers and men behaved like men who are determined to be free.

Yours, most sincerely,
ANTHONY WAYNE.

GENERAL WASHINGTON."

In 1781, he co-operated with General Lafayette, at the South; and was at the capture of Lord Cornwallis, at Yorktown.

In 1795, he succeeded General St. Clair in command of the north-west army, and severely chastised the Indians.

He was satirized by Major Andre, not long before his capture and execution, in a poetical effusion, called the '*Cow Chase,*' the last couplet of which was as follows.—

"And now I've closed my epic strain,
I tremble as I show it,
Lest this same warrior drover Wayne
Should ever catch the poet."

Andre, while under arrest and about to be condemned, penned the following:—

"When the epic strain was sung,
The poet, by the neck, was hung,
And, to his cost, he finds too late,
The dung-born tribe decide his fate."

After having filled many distinguished positions in civil life, he died, in 1796, aged 51 years; and lies buried at Radnor church, in Delaware Co., Pa.; which was erected by Welsh settlers, in 1717, in what was called "The Welsh Tract."

General Daniel Morgan's career, at the head of a brave rifle brigade, during the Revolution, is too well known to require an extended notice.

This "Waggoner General," as he was called, descended from a Welsh family; and was born in New Jersey, in 1737, and at an early age emigrated to Virginia. He was a private soldier in Braddock's expedition. His early occupation was that of a waggoner. He distinguished himself at Quebec with Montgomery and Arnold, and was taken prisoner. After his exchange he was made colonel of the 11th Virginia regiment, in which his own Rifle company was incorporated. His subsequent services were of the most heroic and brilliant character. He performed great services at Stillwater, when Burgoyne was defeated; and by his subsequent victory over Tarleton, at the battle of the Cowpens, in S. Carolina, he gave the first check to the victorious British army in that quarter.

This important victory imparted new courage to the drooping spirits of the patriots, and inspired them with fresh hopes. Congress voted him a gold medal, in token of respect for his services. He served under Gates and Green at the South, and was in many of the hardest fought battles. On one of the flags of his Rifle corps was inscribed, "*Liberty or Death.*" His Rifle company was the first ever organized in the country. He died at Winchester, Virginia, in 1802, aged 67.

General Isaac Shelby, whose ancestors came from Wales, was born in Maryland, in 1750. His profession was that of a surveyor. His services in defence of Liberty were as heroic as they were valuable. He was with his father, Evan Shelby, at Point Pleasant, in 1774 ; and first entered the Continental service as captain of a company of Virginia minute men. He became afterwards attached to the commissary department. One of his most brilliant actions was the defeat of Furgerson at the battle of King's Mountain, when in command of a regiment. He afterwards served with Marion, and was at the battle of Monks' Corner. After having served in the Legislature of North Carolina, he removed to Kentucky, where he assisted in forming its Constitution, and was subsequently Governor of the State.

He again entered the service of the United States, in 1812, at 62 years of age ; and marched to Lake Erie at the head of 6,000 Volunteers, and served during the war with courage, activity, and honor to his country. For his brilliant conduct at the battle of the Thames, Congress voted him a gold medal. He was afterwards offered the office of Secretary of War, by President Monroe ; but he was compelled to decline it, on the ground of his advanced years. He died, in Kentucky, at the age of 76.

General John Cadwallader was of a Welsh family, and born in Philadelphia. He received the appointment of brigadier-general, in 1777 ; and bravely fought at the battles of Princeton, Brandywine, and Monmouth. He fought a duel with General Conway, because he had intrigued with Gates against Washington, and was severely wounded. He afterwards removed to Maryland, became a member of the Legislature, and died, in 1786, aged 43 ; and was wealthy and liberal to a fault.

Major General Charles Lee, who for the greater part of the Revolutionary war was second in command to the commander-in-chief, was born in Wales, in 1731.

He adopted the military profession early in life, and acquired a knowledge of several continental languages. He came to America, in 1756, and distinguished himself in the wars against the French and Indians. He dwelt, for a time, with the Mohawk Indians ; and was made a chief of the tribe under the name, in Mohawk dialect, of "Boiling Water." In 1762, he bore a colonel's commission and served under Burgoyne in Portugal. He returned to England, engaged in politics, and afterwards rambled all over Europe. He met with a favorable reception everywhere, and finally became aid to Poniatowski, king of Poland. He afterwards went with the king's ambassador to Turkey ; and from thence returned, in 1773, *via* Paris to America, and purchased lands in Virginia. Resigning his commission in the British army, he received the appointment of major-general in the Continental service. He was made a prisoner and afterwards exchanged for General Prescott. He had all the Tories of Rhode Island arrested, and rendered many important services before Charleston and in other parts of the country. He was admitted to have been one of the ablest Generals in the Continental army ; and no evidence has ever appeared to show that he was not a sincere and devoted republican. As a Cymro, he loved his race, and boldly denounced king George the Third ; but spoke well of the Prince of Wales. There exists no evidence that he ever aspired to be commander-in-chief ; and the retreat ordered at Monmouth, it was said, arose from a misunderstanding of orders. Washington's mind was, probably, poisoned against him, by those who envied his position and were disposed to look upon him with unjust suspicion. After his suspension from command, in 1780, his republicanism remained to the last. He died in Philadelphia, in the "Slate House," (at one time the residence of Wm. Penn), October 2, 1781, aged 51 ; and was buried in the Christ church burial ground in that city (Episcopal), where also sleep the remains of General Mercer, Captain Anthony Morris, and Dr. Franklin. He died poor. His last words were :—"*Stand by me, Grenadiers!*" The history of his Monmouth trouble remains to be written.

General Morgan Lewis was the son of a native of Wales, and was a well known citizen of New York. He was aid-de-camp to General Gates, at the battle of Saratoga ; and, on the surrender of the English army at that place, was requested by him to receive the sword of General Burgoyne. In Trumbull's picture commemorative of the event, in the rotunda of the Capitol, at Washington, the figure of General Lewis occupies a prominent position.

His honorable military and other public services are too well known to dwell upon. He succeeded George Clinton's first term, as Governor of the State. In 1838, he became President of the Society of the Cincinnati,—an institution founded by Washington,—who was its first President ; having been appointed to fill the vacancy caused by the death of Col. Aaron Ogden, of New Jersey.

He was also the first President of the St. David's Benevolent Society, of New York and Brooklyn ; the members of which hold his memory in grateful remembrance. His portrait hangs in the Governor's room of the New York City Hall ; while his sword, with another portrait, remains in the possession of Daniel L. Jones, Esqr., a member of the St. David's Society.

General Lewis died on the 7th May, 1844, in his 90th year, beloved and respected by all.

General Andrew Lewis was from a Welsh family, and born in Virginia. Himself and five brothers were with Washington when General Braddock was defeated by the French and Indians, and afterwards served during the war of the American

Revolution. He was a major in Washington's Virginia regiment, and was highly esteemed by his commander for his skill and bravery, having commanded at the battle of Point Pleasant, in 1774.

When Washington was appointed commander-in-chief, he recommended Colonel Lewis for the office of major-general; but he was, by some means, overlooked at the time, and accepted the office of brigadier-general. He drove Dunsmore from Gwynn's Island, in 1776. He resigned his commission, in 1780, on account of ill health, and soon after died.

General Wm. R. Davie, though born in England, in 1756, was said to be of Welsh descent, as his name imports. He came to the United States at five years of age, and was adopted by an uncle in South Carolina and graduated at Princeton, in 1776; and soon after commenced the study of Law, at Salisbury, N. Carolina, but abandoned it for the field; and, in 1779, he was attached to Pulaski's Legion, as lieutenant of horse. He headed a cavalry troop at the engagement of Hanging Rock, Ramsey's Mills, and Wahabs' plantation; and was commissary to General Green at the battles of Guilford, Hob Kirk's Hill, and Ninety-six. In 1786, he resumed the profession of Law, having married into the family of General Allen Jones.

General Otho H. Williams, was born in Prince George County, Maryland, in 1768. His ancestors came to that colony from Wales. He was left an orphan at twelve years of age and entered a Rifle corps as lieutenant, when the Revolution broke out, went to Boston under Colonel Cresap, rapidly rose to the rank of major, and fought with distinction at Fort Washington; where he was wounded and captured, and subsequently suffered by the horrors of the Provost Prison, in New York; but was afterwards exchanged for Major Ackland, captured at Saratoga. He then proceeded to take command of a Maryland mounted regiment, and became adjutant to General Green. He covered himself with glory at the battles of Guildford and Eutaw Springs. At the latter place, he led the celebrated charge which swept the field and gained the bloody victory at Eutaw; and opened the gates of Charleston to the Continental troops. Congress conferred on him the rank of brigadier-general. This brave officer died in Maryland, in July, 1794.

General Edward Stephens was of a Welsh family, and a distinguished officer of the American Revolution.

He was a brigadier-general in the Virginia forces, to which State he belonged.

To his consummate coolness and courage at the battle of Guildford may be ascribed the preservation of Green's army, from total route aud ruin. He posted 40 riflemen 20 paces in the rear of his command, and ordered them to shoot down the first man who should retreat from the ranks.

When the militia placed in front precipitately fled, panic-stricken, he preserved the courage of his men, by telling them that they had been ordered to fall back: and opened his lines to let them pass. He then gave the advancing English a *desperate* reception, and was shot through the thigh. His decided movements enabled the regular American troops to stand firm, and to retire in good order from one of the hardest fought battles of the Revolution.

He was, also, in the battles of Great Bridge, Brandywine, and Germantown, and at the siege of York. His whole deportment is said to have been marked by chivalry, benevolence, and nobleness of soul. He died, in 1820, aged 76, without an enemy and lamented by all.

General John Thomas was born in Massachusets, and was of Welsh descent. He distinguished himself in the war, and particularly under Washington before Boston, and took possession of that city on its evacuation by the British. He commenced his military career in the war against the French, and was at the siege of Quebec. While under Washington he occupied Dorchester heights, subsequently became major-general; and died, greatly lamented, with small-pox, at Chambly, Canada, during the progress of the war.

General Joseph Williams descended from a Welsh family, and belonged to Norwich, Connecticut. He took an active part on the patriot side, and subsequently spent much of his time in organizing and disciplining the militia of New London County. He had three brothers in the Continental service,—

Isaac, Frederic, and Benjamin. Frederic was killed in New York, in 1776; and Benjamin died in the Jersey Prison Ship, and was buried in St. Paul's church-yard, in New York.

General Joseph Williams was the father of the late EDWIN WILLIAMS, deceased, who was a worthy and valuable member of the St. David's Benevolent Society; whose amiable disposition endeared him to all its members and to a large circle of friends. His literary labors and attainments were of no ordinary character, and many monuments of his industry in the field of literature remain. At the time of his decease, in the prime of life and manhood, he was engaged in preparing an address on the genius and character of the Welsh people, in which he had made considerable progress. Unfortunately for him and for this Society, this true Cymro was called suddenly from his work and gathered to his fathers.

General Richard Winn was descended from a Welsh family, and was born in Virginia. He entered the patriot service in 1775, and fought at Hanging Rock, where he was wounded. He served with honor during the war, and at its close was appointed first brigadier, and then major-general, of militia; and died in Tenessee, in 1812 or 1813.

We might name other General officers, including Ebenezer Stephens, etc., but we must pass on.

Among the colonels and other subordinate officers, we can only briefly allude to Colonel David Humphreys, who was distinguished during the war, and was both a poet and historian. He entered the field as aid-de-camp to General Putnam, afterwards became aid-de-camp to General Washington, and remained a member of his military family to the end of the war. He often made Mount Vernon his home, and had the unreserved confidence of the General to the end of his life.

He went with Mr. Jefferson to France, as Secretary of Legation, in 1784. For his valor at Yorktown, Congress honored him with a sword. He went as Minister to Portugal in 1790, and to Spain in 1794. He took command of the militia in Connecticut, in 1812; and soon after, died suddenly, of an organic affection.

If time permitted, we could bring to your notice a number of other officers of the rank of colonels, majors, captains, and lieutenants of the Cambrian race, who figured at this eventful period. Among them were Colonel Lambert Cadwallader, Colonel James Williams, who fell at Benington, Captain Rogers, and Captain Anthony Morris.

It may here be remarked, that no Cymry or descendants of Cymry ever turned traitors to the cause they had espoused.

Among the clergymen of Welsh origin, at that period, was the Reverend David Jones, whose life and services were too remarkable to pass over.

His ancestors, on his father's and mother's side, came from Wales and settled, in the last century, on the "Welsh Tract," in Delaware Co., Pa.; but David himself was born in White Clay Creek Hundred, Newcastle Co., in the State of Delaware, in 1736. He was educated for the ministry as a Baptist, and for many years had charge of a congregation in New Jersey. He went as a missionary among the Shawnee and Delaware Indians, in 1772 and 1773. One of his companions, while descending the Ohio in a canoe, was General George Rogers Clarke. Returning from his mission, he espoused the patriot cause: and afterwards settled over a congregation in Chester, Pennsylvania. On the day of a Continental fast and prayer, he preached a sermon before Colonel Dewey's Regiment, and took for his subject:—"*Defensive War in a just cause, sinless.*" It was published and extensively circulated, and did much good in exciting the spirits of the patriots.

In 1776, he received the appointment of chaplain to Colonel St. Clair's regiment, which was ordered to the north-west, and was on duty with the colonel at Ticonderoga, when the enemy was momentarily expected from Crown Point. On Sunday, October 2nd, 1776, before the attack was made, he delivered a characteristic discourse; which produced a powerful effect upon the troops. He urged them, in overpowering strains of eloquence, to put their trust in the God of battles, and in the justice of their holy cause of civil and religious liberty. —All who fell would be remembered as martyrs to freedom, while the love of liberty remained in the breast of man.—He invoked blessings from Heaven on those who should valiantly contend against the foe; and anathemas on those who should faint, fail, or runaway in the hour of struggle; concluding as follows :—"*And may the God of all grace, in whom we live, enable us, in defence of our country, to acquit ourselves like men, to His honor and praise. Amen.*"*

While with General Wayne, he saw an English dragoon alight and go into a house for refreshments—when he went to his horse, took the pistols from the holsters, went into the house, made a prisoner of the dragoon, and marched him into camp—which drew from the General a compliment for the bravery of his minister.

He was chaplain to General Gates and was afterwards with General Wayne, in the Indian campaign to the north-west territory; and was at the massacre of Paoli, where he narrowly escaped death. He was at the battles of Brandywine, Germantown, and Monmouth; and was with the army at Valley Forge, and in all the subsequent campaigns, up to the capture of Lord Cornwallis, at Yorktown.

When the war of 1812 broke out, he again took the field as chaplain, under Generals Brown and Wilkinson, at the age of 76, and served to its close.

His last public act was to address the people at the dedication of the Paoli monument. He died in February, 1820, aged 84, and was buried at the great *Valley church, in sight of Valley Forge* †

Reverend Samuel Davies was a native of Virginia, and became President of Princeton college. Washington's miraculous escape, at Braddock's defeat, caused the Indians to think (who repeatedly fired at him without effect) that he bore a charmed life. Mr. Davies, when speaking before the Volunteer company soon after the battle, used the following prophetic language, in allusion to the then Colonel Washington :—"I cannot but hope, that Providence has hitherto preserved him in so signal a manner, for some important service to his country."

General Washington, in his family associations, was connected in the tenderest ties of relationship with the descendants of Welsh families. His wife, Martha, or "Patsy," as he familiarly called her, was said to have been the grand-daughter

* See his Address in the Appendix.

† See Lossing's Pictorial Field-Book of the American Revolution.

of the Reverend Orlando Jones, who came to Virginia from Wales. Orlando is the continental equivalent for Roland, an old Cambrian name. Colonel Fielding Lewis, of Welsh descent, married his sister; and his son, George Washington Lewis was commander of the General's life guard.

We have seen where the Cymry were in days that "*tried men's souls*." Where are they now? There are, probably, 40,000 or 50,000 natives of Wales in the United States; yet, we know not one of them who holds office under our Government.

Among the 200 or 300 foreign consulates containing appointments from all other civilized nations, and from some that are uncivilized, not a native of Wales appears in the "Blue Book." Why so? Because, next to street-begging, they despise office-begging, as the most degrading to a freeman.

Like Crittenden, they only bow the knee to God, but never to political demagogues for the sake of office. In the language of their historian, Thomas Roscoe, "they know nothing of servility, and as little of arrogance."

They are found at their industrial pursuits—on their farms, in their shops, or at other honest and honorable labor, working out their own independence; but never begging for office or charity, or existing in public alms-houses. With personal liberty, they still adhere to the traditions of their fathers and cherish their ancient love of freedom.

Oh! it would have been a glorious vision to the brave Prince Llewelyn, when life was ebbing through his bleeding wounds, as he sank by treachery into the arms of death, if he could have foreseen, that while the evening sun was shedding its last rays on his native hills, it was then pouring forth its beams in noon-day splendor on a land where his posterity should again unsheath the sword for liberty; and through a long, dark, and bloody struggle, assist in establishing the imperishable principles of civil and religious liberty—principles, cherished for so many centuries among his beloved Cymry, to be afterwards disseminated in other countries.

Fair and lovely Cambria! how fondly thy children love thee—how they linger and hope for thee!

They look to the West for a home—they gaze upon thy smiling valleys—thy pretty villages and neat cottages, beside thy gambolling brooks—it may be, for the last time. The cuckoo's plaintive wail—it may be, is to be heard by them no more. Their little church bell has sounded its last mellow peal for them. Their infantile play grounds, where they sported with wild flowers and listened to the happy tunes of the wandering harper, are about to disappear forever.

They stand, it may be, on the deck of a ship bound to America. As the sun sinks to the west and illumines with its rays, for the last time it may be to them, the distant peaks of Snowdon and Plinlimmon ;—they bid a final adieu to long-cherished memories. Amidst such a sense of bereavement, they have but one consolation left, and that is the thought, that they go to a land of freedom, which the blood of their race was so freely poured out to redeem.

In parting with their native country, they can still exclaim in the language of an exquisite poetess, Mrs. Felicia Hemans, whose home was in Wales :—

"I bless thee ; but, not for the beauty which dwells
In the heart of thy hills, on the rocks of thy shore,
And not for the memory, still deep in thy dells,
Of the bard and the hero, the mighty of yore ;
And not for the songs of those proud ages fled,
Green land ! poet land of my home and my dead.

"I bless thee for all the true bosoms that beat
Where'er a low hamlet smiles up to the skies:
For thy cottage-hearth burning the stranger to greet,
For the love that shines forth from thy children's kind eyes:
May the blessings, like sunshine, around thee be spread,
As I leave thee, thou land of my home and my dead!"

APPENDIX.

[Note 1.]

The preservation of a language in living use among a people, from primitive ages to the present era, affords a strong evidence, that they were never conquered.

"The Welsh have been in possession of a country and its language for 2,400 years, without commixture of any other tongue amongst it; which, perhaps, is the greatest argument that can be given, of a country's never having been entirely subdued by a foreign power."—*See* History of the Society of Ancient Britons, in a letter to his countrymen, by Sir Thomas Jones, K. T. London: 1717.

[Note 2.]

While all the languages spoken in the ages of Greece and Rome have either been corrupted or ceased to have a living, spoken, and written existence, we find the Welsh has been maintained in its native purity and simplicity in the Principality of Wales; where, it is said, to form the daily language of three-fourths of its inhabitants. In their churches in Wales and in America, sermons are preached and hymns are sung, every Sabbath, in the language in which Caractacus addressed Claudius Cæsar at Rome, when carried before him a prisoner in chains, A. D. 51. Tacitus says:—

"On that trying occasion Caractacus alone was superior to misfortune. With a countenance still unaltered—not a symptom of fear appearing—no sorrow, no condescension, he behaved with dignity even in ruin. Being placed before the tribunal on which was seated the Emperor Claudius, he addressed him as follows:—'Had the measure of my success been answerabie to the dignity of my birth and to the greatness of my possessions, I had now entered this city, not as a prisoner but as a friend; nor would you have disdained an alliance with one sprung from illustrious ancestors and the ruler over many nations. My present condition is as glorious to you as it is humiliating to myself. But yesterday I possessed oxen, horses, arms, and riches. Can you wonder that I did not tamely surrender them? If you, Romans, aspire to universal dominion, does it follow that all men must willingly become your slaves? Had I submitted to you without a struggle, neither my own fall nor your success would have been so illustrious. And now should you resolve to put me to death, my story will soon be forgotten. Preserve me, and my name shall live an eternal instance of your clemency."—TACITUS, Annals, lib. xii, chaps. 36, 37.—*See* THACKERAY'S Introduction of Christianity into Britain.

This brave old British warrior fought and defied the Roman power in Britain for nine years, and was by treachery (not by conquest) finally betrayed into the hands of the Emperor.

"Dull as Claudius' feelings usually were, he was struck with admiration" by the bold speech of his prisoner, and ordered his chains to be immediately taken off, and at once pardoned him and all his family.

Mr. Thomas Roscoe in his "*Wanderings and Excursions in Wales*," says, in his Introduction to his first volume, devoted to North Wales, (his second volume being devoted to South Wales)—

"Severe mental toil, like physical labor, is thought to give the truest relish to intervals of enjoyment and repose. Relaxation and pleasure were my chief objects, yet, strange to say, a strange feeling of the fleeting tenure of all human enjoyments filled my heart, as I again bent my steps towards the ancient retreats of British independence. This term is appropriately applied to Wales. It never has been conquered. Its annexation to England in the time of the first Edward, by means of a prince born in Carnarvon; and the descent of the English sovereigns from Catharine, queen of Henry the Fifth, who married Owen Tudor, and whose son was known as the Earl of Richmond, ascended the throne as Henry the Seventh, give to the Cambrians a property in the kingdom, which the Saxons, perhaps, would look for in vain. And it is worthy of remark, that the present Queen of England inherits the *name* as well as the *throne* of a British princess and heroine—Boadicea—the Latinized form of BUDDUG, signifying VICTORIA or VICTORY."

The invasion of the Roman Empire by the northern tribes of Goths and Visgoths, and subsequently of Western and Southern Germany, and finally the eastern portions of England and portions of France, by their Teutonic offshoots known as Saxons and Franks, resembled somewhat the conquest of other branches of the Cymry on the Euxine; including the Greeks farther south by the Turks: with this difference, that the former brought no prophet, religion, or laws with them by which to displace all others existing in the countries they invaded. With improveable intellects, strengthened by free crossing with the Cymry in the north of Europe, or Cimbrioi of the Greeks, or Cimbrii of the Romans, or Cymry of Gaul, Britain, and Scotland, they were disposed to adopt the laws and civilization they found in the countries they overrun. In England they adopted, in the sixth century, the Christian religion, in place of the wooden god, *Woden*; in whose mythology were no less than thirty other deities, male and female, with many absurd and cruel attributes, not unattended by human sacrifices. Their most permanent surviving memento is found in their well-known Gothic architecture, introduced at a later period, and which is more or less copied by all Christian nations in church-building to the present day, but which is unsuitable for other purposes. If the ancient Greeks were earlier civilized than their more northern brethren of the Cambrian race, they were earlier and more hopelessly conquered; first by the Romans, and afterwards by the Turks. Hence, of all the races ethnologically related to or cotemporaneous with the ancient Greeks, the Welsh are the only portion of them which were never conquered, and who at this day retain a country and speak a language which they possessed probably anterior to the fall of Troy or the days of Homer. As links in ethnological science, the ancient Briton or Welsh language and the ancient British laws, form the most interesting study of modern times.

The true key by which to trace out the ethnological distinctions which characterize the inhabitants of the west of Europe, and in this country, is to be found in the study of their languages. And as the Cymric or Ancient Briton is the oldest language extant, as well as the most remarkable for its primitive or radical construction and freedom from admixture with other tongues, though bearing the strongest affinity to the ancient Greek, it must afford one of the best clues to the proper study of ethnology.

To show the identity between the language of Brittany in France and the Welsh, Dr. Owen Pugh, in his chapter on British names, etc., in Vol. II. of his Dictionary of the Welsh Language, relates the following incident :—

"A vessel from Morlaix, in Brittany, being in the Thames, in 1820, the captain was invited to come and hear the harp by the Cymreigyddion. One of the members, after an air had been played, said to the Breton, in Welsh, "Dyna ganu da." To this the Breton, replied, "Na; dyna chware da: canu â genau, a chware â thelyn." So that the Welshman was corrected in his speech by the stranger, thus: "No; that is good playing: it is singing with the voice, and playing with the harp."

In illustration of the origin and character of the Welsh, we take the following interesting paragraph from *Notes and Queries*.

"The Crimea and the Royal Welsh Fusiliers, or 23d Regiment.—Thirty centuries since the Crimea was the hunting-ground of the Cimmerioi, a people who, on the invasion of their country by the Scythians, fought a desperate battle among themselves on the question of resistance or non-resistance; and then, having very probably become *hors de combat*, abandoned the land to the invaders. This circumstance in itself seems sufficient to identify the Cimmerioi with the Celtæ, whose valor was so often and so fatally expended on internal quarrels. This was ever the great error of the Cymry, or Welsh, who thus appear to be one in name and manners with the ancient Cimmerioi. The traditions of the Cymry point to the *Gwlad yr Haf* (Summer Land), or the Crimea, as their original home, and that they emigrated under their leader Hu Gadarn, seeking a land where they could dwell in peace. This evidently alludes to the *Gwlad yr Haf* having become the scene of war and bloodshed; and their wanderings are stated to have continued until their arrival in the Island of Britain. After the revolutions of ages, a mighty expedition has sailed from Britain and landed in the Crimea, and in that expedition some of the descendants of the Cimmerioi have returned to their *mam wlad* (mother-land), where many of them, with that "heroic gallantry" which has conquered on numberless fields of fame have fought and died, and been covered with earth among the barrows of their 'old fathers.'"

The courage and sufferings of this noble Regiment, are feelingly alluded to in the following letter from Gen. Arthur Wynn Torrens, himself of a Welsh family. It is said, that when Gen. Brown saw the deadly charge the Welsh made upon the Russian Battery, he exclaimed, "*Go it my brave Welsh, I will remember you.*"

FIELD OF BATTLE, ON THE RIVER ALMA, CRIMEA, 21st Sept., 1854.

MY DEAR DELME:—I shall wring your heart, indeed, and poor Mrs. Radcliffe's, by the sad intelligence I have, alas, to communicate. Your poor dear boy fell yesterday, at the head of the company which he commanded (No. 1), while gallantly leading them to the attack of a Russian entrenched battery heavily armed, and most strongly occupied. Never was a more noble feat of arms done than the capture of this battery; and in the capture, the poor dear old Welsh were foremost. Their loss has been frightful. Chester, Wynn, Evans, Conolly, my poor sister's boy, Harry Anstruther, Butler, Radcliffe, Young, were all killed dead at the same moment, and within a space of 100 square yards. Applethwaite (it is feared mortally), Campbell, Sayer, Bathurst, Stopton, wounded; only six officers remain untouched, and nearly 200 men are *hors de combat.* The exploit was noble, indeed; but what a sacrifice! The position of the Russians on this river was most formidable; it was defended by 40,000 men, and it was carried in two hours and a half. They lost great numbers, and the conduct of our army, on whom the brunt of the thing fell, was equal to anything that it has ever done. The French behaved admirably. I am heart sick at the loss of so many dear and valued friends, and at the thought of my poor sister's anguish. God alone can comfort us in these overwhelming calamities, and to his Almighty will let us humbly bow. Your dear boy died instantly, without pain, and lies buried in a deep grave along with his comrades, close to the spot where he so nobly died. God bless you Delmé. May He comfort and support you both, is the prayer of your old friend and comrade.

ARTHUR W. TORRENS.

P. S. Harry Torrens and Bulwer buried him. His wound was in the centre of his breast. He lay on his back, and his body had been untouched and respected. God bless and save him. His face was calm, with almost a smile upon it.

A. W. T.

Geographical lines do not change the ethnological character

of a race. They may change its allegiance or citizenship, but not its peculiar traits. Otherwise, the offspring of Africans born in America, would lose their color. The descendants of the Teutonic race, and of that portion of the Irish of Milesian origin, with the offspring of Spaniards, &c., in America, can in most cases be distinctly traced for generations, by their names, and distinguished by physiognomical and other differences of character: the stronger the temperament, the more permanent the race.

As before stated, the true ethnological means of discriminating between a people, is found in their language, and especially in their names for persons and things. Where there is little or no affinity between these, there can be little or no affinity in the races themselves. The primitive geographical names given by the aborigines of a country never change, unless by their complete obliteration by a conquering power. Hence, the ancient British names given to mountains, rivers, lakes, &c., in the greater part of Scotland, Britain, Wales, Cornwall, Armorica, Brittany and Gascony, in France, remain with few corruptions, to the present time. Such is the Avon, Clyde, Ta, or Tayn, Tain, or Thames, (an opening river), Cumbrian mountains, Dundee, Aberdeen, in Britain and Scotland; and Mortaban, Morlaix, &c., in Brittany, France; and which, differ widely from Teutonic, Milesian, Spanish or Saxon names, for similar places or localities. All the west of Scotland, and probably the north of Ireland, according to historical authority, with large portions of other districts in Scotland, were at one time ocupied by the Cymry or branches of this race, who spoke the Welsh, or Cymric language. The river Clyde, pronounced in Welsh "Kluid" (peaceful or quiet), was so named by the Welsh. Aneurin the Welsh poet was born on the Clyde. Also the river Ayr, from the Welsh word *air, bright, clear, etc.* —*See* KNIGHT's Pictorial History of England.

The Welsh alphabet has no K, while C is uniformly sounded as the English K; hence, the Welsh word "cell," is pronounced in Welsh "kell;" and "Celt," is pronounced "Kelt;" which means a wild or covert; and hence, a people like the *Picts* of Scotland, a branch of the Cymry who lived in wild coverts, or wilderness, were called "Kelts." This, being a purely geographical term, has been adopted by persons unacquainted with the Welsh or Cymric tongue, as an ethnological term, and made to embrace dissimilar races in language, habits, laws and customs, in one general race, calling them all "Celts," or "Kelts," after the ancient Greek term Celtæ, of probably the same import.

Again, the Cymric word *Gal*, means a people, who live on a plain, champagne, or prairie country; hence, the Cymric branch who settled in France, were called "*Gauls*," by the Romans. And as an evidence that they were the same people as the Britons, Cæsar mentions that the religion, and customs of the two were similar, and that the latter nniformly were the allies and friends of the Gauls against the Romans; and that in fighting the Gauls he generally found British allies in their ranks sent over from Britain; hence his plea for the necessity of invading the latter.

From the best lights of history, we find that the Cambrian race left the Krimea, and migrated West, passing along the Danube, and by the north of Italy, leaving here and there colonies behind them, one of which was called the Wendi, living on the Elbe, in Lusatia, in Germany, and who speak to this day a slightly corrupted Welsh language, and the Cimbrii, whom the Romans overcame, and whom it is supposed were afterwards commingled with Sclaves and Teutons.* The great body of the Cymry, however, reached the west of Europe. That branch which settled in France were called *Gals* or *Gauls*. Another, who colonized Britain, were called Britons, and those who went to Scotland, and probably to the north of Ireland, at a later period, were called Celts, and afterwards by the Romans, transformed into *Celtedonians* or *Caledonians*.

* The country in Germany occupied more fully, in ancient times by the Wendi, cannot now be very clearly defined. Lusatia embraced the upper branches of the Elbe, and a portion of Prussia, the chief Protestant government in Europe. Bautzen, on the Elbe near Dresden, in Bavaria, and Glogan in Prussia, are said to have been old British towns, with many other old places in the kingdom of Prussia. We understand from a German scholar and antiquarian, that a great many Wendi, or ancient British relicts are shown in the Museums of Dresden and Berlin, and that remains of Druidical altars, exist in various parts of the country. It was supposed that the north of England and part of Scotland, were first peopled by Cymry, who crossed the German ocean, or "Hazy Sea" of the Welsh Triads, from the Elbe.

After the Saxon invasion, a great many Britons emigrated from England to France and joined their countrymen in Brittany, Armorica and Gascony. In the Basque Provinces, and in the vicinity of the Pyrenees, the population is said to be of mixed Welsh descent.—*See* 2d volume of DR. OWEN PUGHE's Dictionary and Grammar of the Welsh language. He says:

"The meaning of '*Celt*' is a covert, from '*Cel*,' a *Shelter*; and it is applied to woody places, as opposed to *Gal*, an open place or plain."

Again, he says, vol. 2, p. 57, in defining the Welsh word, *Gal*:—

"It means a plain or open country. The Cymry, though they were generally careful to preserve their patronymic name, were often called after names of the country they inhabited; the two most universal of which were the open plains and the woods; hence the terms of '*Gal*' and '*Celt*,' with the various subdivisions by which the Cymry were known."

Another branch of the Cymry race were the aborigines of Holland and Belgium, or Flanders. Many Holland names in Geography, and of persons in Flanders, were derived from the Cymry, yet, it has, by its admixture with that of other races of the north of Europe, disappeared there as a living language while it is retained in its full force in Cornwall, Wales, in Brittany, in France, and partially so in Gascony.

The Irish called themselves, before the invasion of King Milesus from Spain, 'Gaoidhel,' in Irish, or 'Gwydhel,' in Welsh, which they pronounce, as if written, 'Goithel,' but the Irish pronounce it 'Gael'; and the Irish, who write on their own history, in this age, says Dr. Pughe, "take the liberty to write the name, 'Gäel,' to the discredit of their history; with a view of identifying the Irish as the descendants of the Gauls. 'Gwydhel' or 'Goithel,' in Welsh means a wild people, living in wild or unsubdued thickets or wilderness of a country."—*See* DR. OWEN PUGHE's work, above referred to.

The Irish language widely differs from the Cymric, and Michael O'Connor, the Irish lexicographer, makes them distinct. The Irish contains a greater number of Latin words than the Welsh; and the chief similarity between them is found in those words which both contain that are similar to Latin words. The Welsh assimilates with the ancient Greek, and contains a large number of words of the same meaning; while the Irish assimilates more to the Latin. This seems strange, because the Romans never held any portion of Ireland, while they were in some portion of Britain for nearly 400 years; and notwithstanding the various invasions of England, the Welsh language is proven by ancient manuscripts and geographical names, as well as by the names of persons and the record of events, to remain essentially the same as that which existed in the time of the Cæsars. The Latin words in the Welsh, or what few of them exist in it, like the Greek and Welsh, are derivative; while the Latin spoken by the Romans, and in a more imperfect form by the Spaniards, from whom the Latin of the Irish was probably chiefly derived, are mostly arbitrary. The Latinized portion of the Irish tongue, was probably carried to Ireland, by King Milesus and his followers, who were called Milesians; and who overrun, it is said, the greater part of the southern and middle portions of the island. Dr. Pughe thinks the Latin words in the Welsh, which are fewer in number than the Greek, were derived from a source anterior to the Romans themselves, and from which the Latins on the Tiber probably obtained it in common with them.

The historical Triads record that the Cymry came to Britain and another colony to Armorica and Brittany from the *Chersonesus Cimbrica*, or Jutland.

"The old name of Hamburg is Treva, and of which, as a Welsh name, the former is a literal translation."—*See* DR. OWEN PUGHE's Dictionary, vol. 2, chapter on British names of places.

Gand or Ghent, in Belgium or Flanders, was probably derived from the common Welsh word "*Gan*," a masculine noun meaning "capacity, the power to contain," or as a preposition, "*Gan*," "by" or "with."

Many Flemish and Dutch names of persons are corruptions from the Welsh; as Hugo for Hughes, from *Hu*, God-like, or the attribute of sky or of heaven: in Scotland called Hugh.

In the Netherlands, the old British names are often modified, by prefixes or terminations, like that of man. Hence "*Hen*," "advanced, experienced, old," is called, "Henman;"

"John," instead of changing to "Jones," as in Wales, is called in the Netherlands, "Johns;" pronounced, however, by them as with us, Jones, but in a harsher form.

[NOTE 3.]

Dyvnwal Moelmud, commonly called by English writers Moelmutius, was said to have lived about three hundred years before the Christian era; and is recorded in the Chronicles as the twenty-first king of Britain. He is said to have been the first to divide the kingdom into commotes or hundreds, for which he is celebrated in the ancient British triads as one of "the three system formers of Britain." Other notices of him appear in the same ancient records, and he is particularly celebrated for having reduced to a system the laws and privileges of the Cymry. This code was extant in the time of Gildas, who translated it into Latin.

Some Institutional and Law Triads, ascribed to Moelmud, are still extant, and are to be found in the Welsh archaeology. An English version of a part of these has recently been published by the *Cymrodorion*, or Cambrian institution, in the first volume of their transactions.—*See* PARRY's Cambrian Plutarch, p. 91.

Dr. Owen Pughe, in his notes to Humphrey Lloyd's "Historie of Cambria," says, that Alfred "translated the ancient laws of Dyvnval Moelmud, king of Britain; and the laws of Marsia, queen of Britain, wife of Cyhelyn, out of British into English." As Alfred acquired a knowledge of Latin and probably did not understand Welsh, these laws were, as hereinafter stated, translated by him from that language into Saxon.

These laws having been compiled and extended over all the Saxon heptarchies by Alfred, were hence called Common Laws, because made to operate over all parts of his kingdom alike.

Asser Manevensis, a Welsh bishop of great learning for his times, was invited by Alfred the Great to reside at his Court, which he reluctantly accepted, and at first only on condition that he might remain six months of each year in Wales.

Asur is the Welsh word for Azure or Blue, or the Sky.—Bardic or Ecclesiastical titles in Wales, in many cases became permanent surnames. Upon this principle Leuver, Morgan, and Bleddyn, celebrated Welsh ecclesiastics, in the 2nd, 3d, and 4th centuries, assumed the names of Lucius, Pelagius, and Lupus; which are but Latin versions of their original appellations. Morgan or Pelagius was the author of the celebrated *Pelagian doctrine or creed,* which gave rise to a bitter religious controversy, and which was condemned as heresy.

While at Alfred's court, Asser is said to have advised the establishment of Oxford University, of which the king was the first provost. He wrote a history of Alfred's reign, and gives no account of his education elsewhere than in England. Neither is there any foundation for such a supposition, in his life by Spelman. Asser while at court made frequent Latin quotations to Alfred, who finally requested him to write them down. He then suggested to Alfred to keep a "Hand-book," which he did; and "Alfred's Manual" or "Hand-book" is still extant. Asser translated Boetius' work on the "Consolations of Philosophy," and was the author of several original works.—*See* Cambrian Plutarch, by PARRY; article, Asser Manevensis.

Asser is said to have translated the ancient British laws into Latin, for Alfred: which he again, as before stated, translated into Saxon, and adopted them as the bases of the English Common Laws.

It was not until the accession of the House of the Tudors to the Throne, or until the reign of Henry the Eighth, in 1544, and after the abolition of the Papal authority in England, that the Welsh would agree to the union. Wales having previously been allowed representatives in Parliament, submitted to taxation and to the extension of the English laws over the Principality.*

Edward the First left Wales independent in her institutions and laws, and secured peace and their alliance by giving them a representative in the Royal family, in the heir apparent to the Throne.

At Rhuddlan Castle, which was built by Llewelyn ap Seisyllt

* For an account of the agency of the Welsh in raising the House of Tudor to the throne of England, *see* Roscoe's Sketch of Rhys ap Thomas, in another part of the Appendix.

in North Wales, may still be seen a huge stone, with the following inscription :—

"THIS FRAGMENT IS THE REMAINS,
Where KING EDWARD the FIRST held his Parliament,
A. D. 1283; in which the Statute of Rhuddlan was enacted—
Securing to the Principality of Wales its Judicial
RIGHTS AND INDEPENDENCE."

Do you call this conquest?

In relation to the contest which prevailed after the invasion of William the Norman, between the advocates of the Justinian Code and the English Common Laws, we refer the reader to the Introduction to Blackstone's Commentaries.

We know that some writers, partial to everything Saxon, have attributed to them credit for bringing into England institutions to which they were never entitled.

If they had brought the principles of the Common Laws or Trial by Jury with them, some traces would have been left in the country on the continent from whence they emanated; such, however, is not the fact. To this day the Trial by Jury is unknown over the greater part of the continent, and in place of the Common Laws, they retain the principles, to a great or less extent, of the centralizing Code of Justinian, so fatal to municipal liberty.

The Trial by Jury was practiced under the ancient British laws centuries before the Saxons were invited over by Vortigern. Before the introduction of Christianity the number of jurors was regulated by the nature of the offence. The higher the position of the accused or the greater the offence, the larger the jury. If a king or prince was to be tried, it required all the dignitaries of the country to sit in judgment. Other persons accused of treason were tried by juries of one hundred, perhaps; and so on down to crimes of less gravity, where the number of jurors would be correspondingly reduced. It was not until after the introduction of Christianity that the number was reduced to twelve, to correspond with the twelve Apostles, which is continued to the present day.

We are disposed to think, that the ancient British mode had many advantages over the present system. We doubt the wisdom of submitting the most important questions of liberty, life, happiness, or property, to twelve men picked up at random, without reference to their intelligence or probity, and believe with the ancient Britons, that the number and intelligence of the jurors should be graduated by the gravity of the offence, and the position of the accused. The Saxons found the trial by Jury and the principles of the Common Law on the Island, when they first invaded it.

Reference has been made in the text of the address, to Oliver Cromwell. We would here state, that his real name was Williams, and that he was related to Roger Williams, the founder of Rhode Island. His name, it is said, was changed to Cromwell, the name of his mother's family, to enable him to inherit some property. There were a number of Welshmen of rank who aided Cromwell in his establishment of the Commonwealth, among them were John Jones, Thomas Harrison, Hugh Peters, and John Hews.on, who voted, as members of Parliament, for the execution of Charles I., and were afterwards beheaded as regicides. The Hon. Benj. F. Butler of New York, late Attorney General of the United States, is the lineal descendant, on his mother's side, of John Jones; and the late President, Wm. Henry Harrison, was a descendant of the regicide, Thomas Harrison.

In again referring to the ancient institutions of Wales, we may remark that the Welsh have no name for Prince, as the English understand the word; those called Princes in English, were simply called leaders, and were elective by the people; not princes by the right of blood alone, for they could be set aside and others substituted in their places. Their kings were also elective.

The descent of land in Wales, was allodial, or in fee. The feudal tenure did not prevail fully, until after its union with England. And even at the present day, in some of the interior counties, the allodial title to lands is said to be set up in the courts in opposition to the feudal tenure. Church tithes, introduced among the Saxons by Theodoric, Bishop of Canterbury, between 668 and 690, under the Saxon kings of the Heptarchies, and which are referred to in another note, were unknown in Wales for centuries afterwards.

We have alluded to Wm. Penn. We would state, that a

large number of his followers were Welshmen. And the beautiful and refined city of Philadelphia contains a larger proportion of Welsh descendants, than any other city in America. The first Mayor of the city was Anthony Morris, and the first Governor of the colony of Pennsylvania was Thomas Lloyd, who were both Welshmen. The literature, science, and patriotism of Philadelphia, has exerted a favorable influence over the country generally.

Of late years, Welsh immigration has been chiefly directed to the western portions of Pennsylvania and New York, and also to Ohio, Illinois, and Wisconsin. Cambria county in Pennsylvania, was chiefly settled by Welsh; also Oneida county in New York, one of the most flourishing counties in the interior of the State. Beyond the town of Utica, with a large mixed population, it is said, that there is not a poor house in existence in the county.

[NOTE 4.]

The Reverend Francis Thackeray, A. M., formerly of Pembroke College, Cambridge, in his researches into the Ecclesiastical and Political state of Ancient Britain, arrives at the conclusion, that if Christianity was not carried into Britain by the preaching of St. Paul himself (regarding which authorities differ) its first promulgation was made in the Island by some of the immediate disciples or followers of the Apostle of the Gentiles.

"In all probability the churches in Gaul or Britain were founded about the same period, and we have reason to believe that Christianity was preached in both countries before the close of the first century.

"The result of my investigations on my own mind has been the conviction that, about A. D. 60, in the life-time of St. Paul, a church existed in Britain, consisting of Bishops, Deacons, and lay members; and which, by slow degrees, extended itself widely through the country. That it administered the Holy Sacraments of Baptism and the Lord's Supper according to the Divine command of the Apostolic usage, and that it was independent of foreign jurisdiction."—*See* page 12, Preface of THACKERAY's work on the introduction of Christianity into Britain; also p. 87 of his Text.

Pomponia Grecina, an illustrious lady, wife of Aulus Plau-

tius, from Britain, and who lived at Rome in the life-time of St. Paul, was supposed to have embraced Christianity, and died in A. D. 83.

Claudius Rufina, the wife of Pudens, who lived at Rome in the life-time of St. Paul, was said, with her husband, to have been Christians. She was either born in Britain or was the daughter of British parents. She took a lively interest in the introduction of Christianity into the Island, and was spoken of by Martial in the following lines :—

> "Claudia! of azure-painted Britons born
> What Latian wit and Latian grace adorn;
> Such forms might Rome among her daughters place,
> And Attic matrons deem of Attic race."

—MART., lib. xi., Epig. 54. *See* THACKERAY, vol. 1, p. 96.

Again, in allusion to the marriage of Claudia to Pudens, Martial says ;—

> "Oh! Rufus Pudens, whom I own my friend
> Has ta'en the foreign Claudia for his wife;
> Propitious Hymen! light thy torch and send
> Long years of bliss to their united life"

—*Ibid.*, lib. iv., Epig. 12.

From other lines it appears that Martial's verses afterwards assumed a more serious character, through respect to the religious feelings of both Pudens, his father and his wife. Mr. Thackeray identifies Pudens and Claudia with the persons alluded to by St. Paul, in his second Epistle to Timothy :—

"Eubulyus greeteth thee, and Pudens and Linus and Claudia, and all the brethren."—2 *Tim.* iv. 21.

Linus became the first Bishop (not Pope) of Rome, after the death of St. Peter. At the time Martial wrote he was between 30 and 40 years of age, and might well have been acquainted with the two individuals named in the same sentence with Eubulyus and Linus, A. D. 67.—*See* THACKERAY, vol. 1, p. 99.

Some authorities of great weight prove very conclusively that Christianity was introduced into Britain some years earlier than the period stated by Mr. Thackeray. Without designating with certainty the names of its first promulgators we have reason to believe that the first churches established in Britain were in South Wales ; aud that those who introduced Christianity came over from France to that part of Britain. For centuries the stronghold of the primitive church was at St. David's, and some other places of note in South Wales.*

The Saxons did not land in England until A. D. 477. McFarlane, in Knight's History of England, says :—

"At the period of their invasion of Britain the Saxons were as rough and uncouth as any of the barbarian nations that overturned the Roman Empire."

About 200 years intervened from their first landing, in 477, before they established themselves in that part of England known as the Saxon Heptarchies.

St. Augustine, who was sent over by Gregory to convert the Saxons, did not land in England until the year 597, after the Britains had been already in possession of Christianity for 437 years.

The first convert of St. Augustine, was Ethelbert, king of Kent (" *Cantawra*" in Welsh, hence Canterbury). This monk was the Austin, as called by the Welsh, who visited the primi-

*" There is a chapel dedicated to St. TECLA, near the mouth of the River Wye, South Wales, said to have been erected in the year 47. It has been covered by the sea, but the remains are yet visible at some distance below high-water mark ; an instance that the sea encroaches upon the Monmouth shore and Glamorganshire coasts, while on the Flintshire and Cheshire shores (North Wales), much land has been gained from the sea.

"In the chancel of Mathern church, of British origin, near the confluence of the Wye and Severn, is a tomb erected by Bishop Godwin, decorated with ornaments and military emblems to the memory of Theodore, King of Glamorgan, with this inscription :—

"HERE LIETH ENTOMBED THE BODY OF THEODORIC,
King of Morganwg or Glamorgan, commonly called St. Thewdric, and Accounted a martyr, because he was slain in battle against
The Saxons (being then Pagans) and in defence of the Christian religion.
The battle was fought at Tintern, where he obtained a great victory. He died
Here, being on his way homeward, three days after the battle, having given
Order to Maurice (Morris) his son, who succeeded him in the kingdom,
'That in the same place he should happen to decease, a church
Should be built and his body buried in the same, which
Was accordingly performed, in the year 600.'"

—*See Tourist in Wales*, with Historical and Topographical Notices, page 84. George Virtue · London and New York.

tive churches of Wales, and endeavored to influence St. David and other Welsh Bishops, to acknowledge the usurped supremacy of the Pope of Rome, spiritual and secular; to which they offered the most determined and decided refusal. Their resistance to the claims of the Papacy, led afterwards to the most sanguinary wars between the Saxons and the Welsh; the latter manfully struggling for centuries in defence of their civil and religious liberties.

The reader is referred to "*The History of the Rise and Progress of the Society of Ancient Britons.*" By Sir THOMAS JONES, Kt., in a letter to his countrymen, published in London, 1717. The author says that—

"This being the society (Ancient Britons) of an entire principality, consisting of thirteen counties; whose inhabitants of all degrees and orders, have ever been famous in story for their generosity, valor, and bravery.

"And as the princes and noblemen of Wales, have not been more conspicuous in the generous and steady defence of their ancient civil rights and liberties, than have been their archbishops and bishops, in supporting and maintaining the true primitive Christianity and the ancient rights of their sees. For there was in Wales an Archbishop of *Caerleon-upon-Usk*, in Monmouthshire, and afterwards at *St. Davids*, long before Pope Gregory sent Austin (called St. Augustine in English), hither to convert the Saxon king *Ethelbert*, to the Christian faith.

"And though upon his coming hither, the good old *British* Bishops were willing to pay *Austin* a civil respect, and to advise with him about the common cause of Christianity in general; yet they bravely withstood all his pretentions to any SUPERIOR JURISDICTION OVER THEM, and denied that the POPE, or *any foreign Prince or Prelate, had any right or authority to invest* AUSTIN *with any such* POWER.

"And, as they had received a more pure faith, probably by the preaching of St. Paul himself, the great Apostle of the Gentiles; so they still continued their ancient customs and rights, and kept their churches clean and untainted from the infection of idolatry, and from all usurpation of the see of Rome.

"And the great St. David's courage in this affair was equal to his birth and piety, and he and his successors, continued their Welsh metropolitan jurisdiction up to the time of Edward I."

St. David was not canonized, until it was done by Pope Calixtus the II., about 500 years after his death. Notwithstanding this, he never was a Roman Catholic or acknowledged, during his life, the authority of the Pope of Rome.*

It has been remarked "That Popery entered Saxon England like a Lamb, but soon grew up to be a roaring and devouring Lion;" while Wales, amidst cruel wars in self-defence, remained firm in the faith of the primitive church.

The taxation of the people by tithes commenced with and were claimed by the clergy to have been granted by charter, under Ethelwulf, king of Mercia, in 865, which became general over England under all the Saxon kings of the Heptarchies. These, at first, were small, but soon became immense. The clergy at first were content to preach in wooden houses and travel from place to place; which, under the influence of wealth, soon gave way to splendid stone edifices and luxurious and licentious livings. The gifts of the rich were encouraged, by which means they were to expiate their crimes and secure happiness in Heaven. The influx of wealth engendered corruption, and monasteries and other recluse establishments were infected with the general degeneracy that prevailed. The eagerness of the great to bestow costly gifts on the churches became so general that finally King Edward, known as the weak Confessor, was persuaded by Norman priests, among whom was Robert of Canterbury, to give away his kingdom to William the Norman.† The wealth and corruption of the Church caused a great deal of civil war and blood-shed in England.

As Wales was exempted from tithes until after her union

* St. Patrick is shown by the most conclusive historical records to have been a Briton by birth, and it is immaterial whether he was born on the Clyde, in Scotland, in the north of France, or south of Wales. At the time of his birth and ministry, the Saxons had not invaded England, and the Welsh inhabited the banks of the Clyde.

Camden says, he was born in Rhoss, Pembrokeshire, Wales, and his father was Calfurnius, a Welsh priest, and his mother was sister to St. Martin, of Tours in France. Alexander Hugo, says, that he was a Briton, and born in the British Province of Armorica in France. (See *Camden's Briton*, Article Pembrokeshire. See *Alexander Hugo's Celtic Monuments*, vol. 1.)

St. Patrick, some historians say, went to Ireland from South Wales, in about the year 400. Others say he went from the Clyde. In the wall which surrounds St. David's Cathedral, South Wales, on the site of one of the oldest churches in Britain, there is a gate called *Porth Patrick's*, to this day.

† *See* KNIGHT'S History of England, abridged by the Author, vol. 2, pp. 37—39: Article, the Saxon Period

with England, she was to a great extent, free from the corruption in her churches to which the system had led in England; and which had aided so greatly in building up a powerful religious Hierarchy, that remains an incubus upon the industry and liberty of the people to the present day.

The population and religious condition of Wales at the present time, is shown by the following statement, taken from the English *Nonconformist* Newspaper of 1854.

The census, in 1851, gave a population of 1,188,914. In the same year the Nonconformists or Independents—such as Baptists, Methodists, Presbyterians, Congregationalists, etc.—were shown to have had in North Wales, 1,238, and in South Wales, 1228; total, 2,466 chapels; being 2,048 more than they had in 1801, and 1,487 more than the churches of the Established Church. The unendowed Protestant sects (as above), have furnished not less than 680,418 sittings; or within a small fraction of the whole accommodation required by the people. The figures being 57.2 per cent. This provision for attendance was not neglected by the population. On the census Sunday the aggregate number of persons who attended these churches amounted to 687,141; or an average attendance during the day of nearly every person able to do so. Thus carrying out their independence in their voluntary support of a free church, while taxed to support the established religion.

The good order and freedom from crime in Wales are as remarkable as their love of independence in their churches and other matters.

Wales not only defended her own soil against religious oppression, but the earlier reformers found a refuge and protection in her borders, where they lived in peace, and free from persecution. Among these were the Lollards and Wickliffites, and also Jeremy Taylor, who wrote some of his ablest compositions in South Wales.

To this day, Wales is the bee-hive of radical Protestantism in Europe. It was this kind of Protestantism, which did so much to animate patriotic minds during our revolutionary war, and which has since tended to keep alive free education, and devotion to our free institutions.

The ancient Greeks and the Cymry resembled each other

not only in their language but also in their early mythology, bardism, &c. The emblem of eternity with the Greeks was a circle. So was that of the Druids. Their Druidical Temples, such as Stonehenge, were erected in concentric circles, if you please, representing an eternity within an eternity, in the innermost of which, men's remains were interred in stone coffins. The Greeks connected their religion with Astronomy and Philosophy, so did the Druids Their long robes were white, emblematical of truth and holiness. The Bards, another order, wore sky blue robes, significant of the firmament, or purity. They worshipped amidst their vast circular altars, or amidst spreading oaks and in secluded valleys, at the base of frowning mountains.

The Greeks had romances and dialogues, so had the Britons. Pythagoras, who was the first that taught that the earth was round and revolved around the sun, on its own axis, 539 years before the Christian era, believed in the transmigration of souls. The Druids also taught the transmigration of souls.

"The introduction into the Greek Philosophy of the doctrine of the metempsychosis is commonly attributed to Pythagoras; and there are various passages in ancient authors which make mention of, or allude to some connection between that philosopher and the Druids. Abares, the Hyperborean, is by many supposed to have been a Druid, and he, Iamblicus tells us, was taught by Pythagoras to find out the science of numbers. The Grecian Philosopher derived his philosophy from the Druids. A report is preserved by Clement of Alexandria that Pythagoras, studied under both the Druids and the Brahmins."—*Strom.* 135. *See* KNIGHT's History of England; article, British and Roman period of England.

It has been conjectured that the fundamental principle of the Druidical esoteric, or secret doctrine, was the belief in one God.

"Diogenes Laertius acquaints us, that the substance of their system of faith and practice was comprised in three things, namely, to worship the gods, to do no evil, and to behave courageously."

Druidism was said to have been taught to the greatest perfection in Britain. It had its head quarters in Anglesey. Here exist, one place which is called Myfyrion, "The place of Studies;" a second place called Caer Edris, "The city of Astronomers;" and a third place called Cerrig Brudyn, or "The Astronomer's Circle."

To master its doctrines so as to become a Druid of rank required a study of twenty years, after time had frosted their long and flowing beards. They were said to have existed in Britain for more than a thousand years before the birth of Christ. In their system they embraced the study of Natural Philosophy, Astronomy, Geometry, Jurisprudence, Medicine, Poetry, and Rhetoric ; besides, Arts of Magic and Astrology.

"They were not mere professors : Cicero, Cæsar, Pliny, Tacitus, Diodorus Siculus, Strabo, and others, all speak with respect of the acquirements of the Druids.

"Mr. Theophilus Jones, in his history of Breconshire, denies that the Druidical faith imposed human sacrifices ; and that persons executed during their ceremonies were the grosser criminals."—*See* Davies on the Mythology of the British Druids.

The transmigration of souls, which they taught, was said to have been invented to prevent the commission of crime. Thus, if a man lived the life of a drunken loafer, he would enter the body of a dirty pig. If his vices were of a grosser nature, he would enter a still more repulsive animal. On the contrary, should he possess a kind and gentle disposition, he might enter a gazelle or a dove ; if a warrior, the body of a lion ; if of a lofty genius and elevated soul, the body of an eagle. Such a doctrine would tend to prevent a man from making himself a "Hog" in this life, for fear of becoming a "Grunter" hereafter.

We have alluded to the strong religious antagonistic characteristics of the Queens Mary and Elizabeth. As an illustration of the same, we give the following incident from Roscoe's Sketches of Wales, which occurred at Chester, formerly an old Welsh town :—

"Dr. Cole, a commissioner in the time of Queen Mary, and a zealous Roman Catholic divine, was proceeding to Ireland, with a secret warrant against the Protestants of that country, and stopped one night at Chester. The mayor in his municipal character waited upon him, and he unguardedly spoke of the cruel business in which he was engaged, and took out his commission in the presence of his hostess, who had a brother, of that communion, in Dublin. When the mayor left him, he politely attended him down stairs, and the hostess in the mean time took the important document from the box, and substituted in its place a pack of cards, with the knave of clubs placed uppermost. The doctor on his return, perfectly unconscious of what had been done, put up the box, and on his arrival in the Irish metropolis, presented it in form at the castle, in presence of the lord deputy and the privy council, purposely assembled to examine its momentous contents. His lordship opened it, and the whole party, as well as the commissioner himself, were in the utmost astonishment and consternation to see the knave of clubs make his appearance amidst the solemn conclave, without any script to account for his knave's face at that unwelcome moment. Cole, burning with mortification, assured the assembly that the box *had* contained a commission, but why it was not there, and how the cards came into its place, he was as ignorant as they. Disappointed and chagrined he returned to the English court, and being in high favor with Mary, soon obtained a fresh commission; but before he could again arrive in Ireland, the queen died. The name of this bold and quick-witted woman was Elizabeth Edmunds (of a Welsh family), and her namesake, the good Queen Bess, when she came to the throne, hearing of this adroit stratagem, rewarded the woman with a pension of forty pounds a year for her life. To this act was owing, probably, the safety of the Protestants of the "Green Isle."—Vol. 1, page 12.

As an illustration of the merry lives which monks lived in the olden time, we annex the following facetious lines from Owain's (a Welsh poet) description of the hilarity of the monks of Valle Cruces, on the borders of Wales. He died in its vicinity not long after, and the monks out of revenge refused him burial in their church-yard. Roscoe says this was a wealthy institution, which may be judged of by the magnificent hospitality used by the monks; who are described by Owain as having a table usually covered with four courses of meats, served up in silver dishes, with sparkling claret for their general beverage.

"Many have told of the monks of old
What a saintly race they were;
But 'tis most true that a merrier crew
Could scarce be found elsewhere;
For they sung and laughed,
And the rich wine quaffed,
And lived on the daintiest cheer.

"And the abbot meek, with his form so sleek,
Was the heartiest of them all,
And would take his place with a smiling face,
When the refection-bell would call;
And they sung and laughed,
And the rich wine quaffed,
Till they shook the olden wall."

We have, in another part of the Appendix, made allusion to the Eastern or Caucasian origin of the Cymry; if space permitted, many other proofs could be adduced.

The old British words were remarkably expressive of the physical traits that appertained to places. The derivation of ancient geographical terms, taken from Dr. Owen Pughe's Welsh and English Dictionary, proves the great antiquity of the Welsh language as well as the origin of the Welsh people.

Hence, *Caucasus* is derived from the Welsh words which at this day stand in the Welsh dictionary, as "*Cau*," to shut up, to fence in, to encompass, and "*Cas*," separated, insulated.

The Caucasian chain of mountains stretches from the Black Sea to the Caspian, forming an immense barrier between Europe on the north and Asia to the south. What term could more perfectly express the position and character of the Caucasus than the ancient British word of "*Caucas*," a barrier, to shut up—like a gate, to enclose Europe from Asia? *Caucasus* is a name this mountain chain has borne from the earliest human records, and was so called before the days of ancient Troy.

Again, the *Caspian Sea* is derived from the Welsh word, "*Cas*," separated, insulated, and "*Pen*," head: literally, a sea with a head or source, but insulated and without an outlet. What name could better express this great insulated salt-water sea?

A tribe of people (probably Cymric) residing on its shores, were called *Caspens* or *Caspii* by the ancient Greeks.

Many of the names of places in Servia and in what is now Turkey in Europe are, with slight corruptions, recognised in their derivation from British words, which are still preserved in the Welsh language. Thus "*Marmora*," applied to the sea near Constantinople, is found in the Welsh words "*Marm*," dead, and "*Mor*,"sea; meaning, as its name imports, *Dead Sea*;

from the quiet state of its waters, being land-locked and with little fall or rise in its tides.

Again, "*Morea*" may be in part derived from "*Mor*," the sea, joined to "*Area*," space or territory in the sea; or meaning a peninsula. Again, "*Crimea*" comes from the Welsh word "*Crymu*," pronounced "*Krime*;" the C being sounded as K, and the u as e; which means "to bend, to curve, or circular," literally, a circular peninsula; which fully applies to the Crimea: the *a* is probably a Latin termination.

The Balkan or ancient *Hæmus* chain of mountains is derived from the Welsh words "*Bal*," a high or lofty peak or peaks and "*Can*," brightness or whiteness, etc.; literally, white mountains; and its other name of *Hæmus*, comes from "*Hem*," a a border, or very expressively, a border chain of mountains.

Again, *Albania*, *Alban*, etc., comes from the Welsh word "*Alban*," compounded of "*Al*," the root of a number of Welsh words, and which means most high, elevated, angelic, most, utmost, etc; and "*Ban*," high, lofty. Scotland was called "*Alban*," from its extreme northern limits or mountainous character; which, ultimately, became the name of the whole country, under the title of *Alban*. Hence the derivation of Albany, and of St. Albans, in England. "*Danube*" was probably derived from "*Dan*," under, below, and "*Uf*," pronounced "*Uv*" or "*Ub*," spreading or diffused.

The *Alps* was probably derived from "*Al*," grand, sublime, or lofty, and "*Pen*," head. The *Carparthian* mountains, from "*Car*," close, compact, and "*Parth*," a division, or a parting; in other words, a dividing chain of mountains. To this day, they separate Hungary from the countries north and west of it.

Moravia comes from "*Mor*," sea, and "*Af*," pronounced *Av*, progress, going forward from the sea. or distant from the sea.

The *Save*, a tributary of the Danube, comes from "*Saf*," *Sav*, standing, slow, or quiet river.

Some writers suppose that another branch of the Cymry went eastward from the Caucasus, and penetrated as far as India. The Institutes of Menu, translated by Sir Wm. Jones, in many respects bear a resemblance to the ancient British laws compiled by Dyfnval Moelmud.

"*Menw*" in Welsh, pronounced *Menu* or *Menoo*, means

the seat of the soul. The Institutes of Menu or Brahmin Laws, translated by Sir Wm. Jones, (himself the son of a native of Wales) contain some of the principles of the ancient British laws. Though greatly expanded into superstitious creeds and statutes and clothed in verbose language. The former are much more simple and practicable. They are written in brief paragraphs, something after the fashion of the ancient British Triads. Sir Wm. Jones says:—

"The name '*Menu*' is clearly derived from *Menses*, *Mens*, or mind; as all the Pandits agree that it means 'intelligent.'"

"*Tan*," in Welsh, means to spread out; hence, some have perhaps, on no very good authority, supposed that Affghanis*tan*, Hindos*tan*, etc, may have been derived from an ancient wandering tribe of the Cymry, who went to the south and eastward from the Caucasus.

Among the sections of country said to have been settled by the Cymry were, the valley of the Arno, in Italy; including Genoa on the north, and the islands of Elba and Corsica off the coast. called *Etruscans* and *Ligurians*, hence the name of Leghorn. The river Loire in France is said to have been derived from *Liger* or *Ligur*, from the Cymric tribe who settled on its shores. Tours, on its banks, it is possible came from "*Towyr*," pronounced *Tour*; and Nantz, near its mouth, comes from the Welsh word "*Nant*," a hollow, formed by water. This town was the ancient capital of Brittany, in France, where was proclaimed the celebrated edict of toleration, afterwards revoked by Louis XIV.

Before closing, we would briefly allude to the genius of the Welsh for invention. It is said, that a people who make no inventions or discoveries make no progress. The records of the English and American Patent Offices bear abundant evidence of the invention of Welshmen and their descendants; still we intend to be very brief, being confined by our limits, and can only refer to a few instances.

WM. EDWARDS was a native of Glamorganshire, South Wales, and was a self-taught Engineer, his education, at first, having only extended to a knowledge of reading and writing in his native language. Born near the deep and rapid mountain-stream of the River Taff, he conceived the idea of bridging it. The river had a rapid course through a deep valley, and was subject to sudden and powerful freshets. He constructed a bridge of a beautiful and elegant form, of three arches, over the river, which during a sudden flood was carried away.

He then began a second bridge, and constructed it of hewn stone, of a single arch of 140 feet span, from pier to pier; which he completed in 1751, having only to add the parapets, when a tremendous freshet came and carried it away also.

He then commenced a third bridge, which he finished in 1755; nine years from the commencement of his first labors. By adopting cylindrical holes in what are called the haunches of the bridge, he increased its strength and elegance. This bridge is standing to the present time, just 100 years old; and maintains its span, in a single arch, of 140 feet.

At the time of its erection it was the largest stone arch in the world. He, afterwards, built several other important bridges in Wales and England, which formed the models for several of the London bridges. A nephew of his, taught by him, built the Newport bridge, which is still standing.

He was also a farmer, and officiated on Sundays as a Pastor to an Independent congregation. He accepted the usual salary; but, instead of putting it in his pocket, he returned it all and more besides, to the poor. He continued to labor and to preach to the end of his days, and died at the age of 70.

THE FIRST INVENTORS AND PATENTEES OF THE LOCOMOTIVE ENGINE.

"'The first practical application of the Steam Engine, as a locomotive power, took place in 1804, on a railroad at *Merthyr Tydvil*, Glamorganshire, South Wales.

"The engine was constructed by Messrs, Trevithic and Vivian, (both Welshmen, the latter name being a transformation from '*Vychan*,' little, or Vaughan in English) under a Patent obtained by them, two years previously, (or in 1802).

"This engine, in several respects, resembled in form and in structure those which have since been used for a like purpose."—*See* Brande's *Encyclopedia*; Article, Locomotive.

Oliver Evans, of Philadelphia, was the poor boy of a Welsh farming family in Pennsylvania, and self-taught. He invented the *High Pressure Steam Engine*, without the use of which the Mississippi river, owing to its perpetual muddy water could never have been successfully navigated. It was found the sediment of the water chocked up or wore the sliding valves of the low pressure engines.

In 1804, he made a proposition to the *Lancaster Turnpike Company* for the construction of Steam-engines and Carriages to transport merchandise and produce between Philadelphia and Columbia; and went into figures to show its feasability and probable profits.

The following extract from his Memorial will be read with interest:—

"I might as well have made this improvement about twenty years ago, when I first conceived the means by which it is to be affected. But prudence has compelled me to suspend my natural inclination and capacity for invention, and confine my improvements to such things as I was immediately interested in. During the Revolution I made wire, wool, and cotton cards. My improvements in those arts exceeded all known here at that time. I have no doubt but that my engine will propel both against the current of the Mississippi, and wagons on our turnpike road with great profit."

The Editor of the *Philadelphia Enquirer* of April 6th, 1855, says:—

"We have been shown a manuscript endorsed by Oliver Evans, and probably written by one of his family, in which is given a detailed account of the invention of steamboats. He states that in 1775 or 1776 he conceived the idea of propelling boats with his engines, by means of wheels at the sides, and communicated his discovery to others—namely, to George Latimer, in 1777, and to Evan and Joseph Evans, both of whom were then living to testify. In 1784, he matured in idea and by experiments, a Steam-engine applicable to the purpose of propelling carriages and boats so far, that he petitioned the State Legislatures, in 1786, to secure to him the right of propelling land-carriages, and obtained Acts of the Legislatures of Maryland and New Hampshire.

"The document from which the above extract is taken, is quite voluminous, but deeply interesting, and we hope to be able to give it at length at some future time."

JAMES WATT, the inventor of the *Low Pressure Engine*, was born on or near the *Clyde*, in Scotland; whose name was, probably, an abbreviation of *Watkins*, a Welsh name.

FOX TALBOT, the discoverer and improver of Photographs on paper, is said to be of Welsh descent, on the female side.

SIR HUMPHREY DAVY was born of poor parents, at Penzance, in Cornwall: and was (as both his names import) of Ancient Briton stock.

DR. THOMAS P. JONES, at one time at the head of the U. States' Patent Office and Editor of the Journal of the Franklin Institute, was born in Breconshire, Wales.

We could name many other Cymry or their descendants, who have made important discoveries and inventions, but we must draw to a close.

The Welsh and their descendants, though mostly devoted to useful and solid improvements in manufacturing industry, yet have supplied many persons of distinction in the fine arts. Many important improvements adopted in mining operations and in the vast iron works of Wales, as well as in the great machine and mill works of England, attest their inventive ingenuity.

MR. GIBSON, who is at present the most eminent sculptor in England, is a native of Wales. Many painters of Welsh origin or descent have also contributed works of art, which have ornamented the galleries of England and America.

INIGO JONES was of a Welsh family and the immediate predecessor of SIR CHRISTOPHER WREN. He was the architect of White Hall Palace, London, and of many other noble structures which to this day stand in the "West End," as monuments to his genius.

OWEN JONES is well known as the ornamental architect of the Crystal Palaces of Hyde Park and Sydenham.

In the modern walks of Science, we have Professor OWEN of the Royal College of Surgeons; the learned zoologist, and in comparative anatomy, the Cuvier of his age.

Notices of this description could be multiplied if our limits permitted.

The smallness of a population or geographical extent of a country does not affect the merits of a people. The Principality of Wales is not as large as many of the States comprising the Union; being only about 150 to 175 miles in its greatest length North and South, by about 80 or 90 miles wide, as at present bounded.

It is not the *number* or *quantity* of a people which constitutes their true greatness, but their *quality*.

If Wales had been powerful in extent of country and in numbers, her long and noble struggle against merciless and marauding invaders, for so many centuries, would have won her less renown Differing from other countries, she never enriched herself by the robbery of those she overcame. This little nation fought in a thousand battles for home and liberty.

There was more real manhood in the 300 Greeks, with Leonidas, at Thermopylæ, than there was in the 100,000 Persians, under Xerxes; and more real power of mind, and all that constitutes the true nobility of man, in the small community of Attica, in Greece, than existed, at that age, in all the rest of the world.

For thousands of years the vast Scythian hordes and their off-shoots have been at war with the Cymric or Caucasian races. They followed them from the Caucasus and the Crimea to the west of Europe, and were again attacked by their descendants in the Goths, and their offspring. These wars, which led to the final conquest of Greece and Rome, put back the civilization of Europe for more than five centuries. Scythian or Tartar hordes still swarm from their vast northern hive, and are at this moment, with their ancient courage, waging war against the Briton and the Gaul.

The watchwords of the Scythians have ever been, "*Conquest and Plunder.*"

The Caucasian races have had enemies among the darker mixed races of northern Africa, on the south; but, beyond their temporary conquest of Sicilly and parts of Spain, where traces of their race remain, their influence on the destiny of the more northern Caucasian races has been less marked.

While the Cymry have had to defend themselves against outsiders, they have greatly damaged each other by intestine wars.

The long contests which have raged between England and

France, in which the descendants of the same race were brought into the field, were conducted with all the ill-blood and ferocity of civil wars.

ADDRESS OF REV. DAVID JONES,

TO GENERAL ST. CLAIR'S BRIGADE, AT TICONDEROGA, WHEN THE ENEMY WERE HOURLY EXPECTED;

October 20, 1776. (*Referred to in the Address.*)

"My Countrymen, Fellow-soldiers, and Friends:—

"I am sorry that during this campaign I have been favored with so few opportunities of addressing you on subjects of the greatest importance both with respect to this life and that which is to come; but what is past cannot be recalled, and now time will not admit an enlargement, as we have the greatest reason to expect the advancement of our enemies as speedily as Heaven will permit. [The wind blew to the north, strongly.] Therefore, at present, let it suffice to bring to your remembrance some necessary truths.

"It is our *common faith* and a very just one too, that all events on earth are under the notice of that God in whom we live, move, and have our being; therefore we must believe that, in this important struggle with the worst of enemies, he has assigned us our post here at Ticonderoga. Our situation is such that, if properly defended, we shall give our enemies a fatal blow, and in great measure prove the *means* of the *salvation* of North America.

"Such is our present case, that we are fighting for all that is near and *dear* to us, while our enemies are engaged in the worst of causes, their design being to subjugate, plunder, and enslave a free people that have done them no harm. Their tyrannical views are so glaring, their cause so horribly bad, that there still remain too much goodness and humanity in Great Britain to engage unanimously against us, therefore they have been obliged (and at a most amazing expense, too) to hire the assistance of a barbarous, mercenary people, that would cut your throat for the small reward of sixpence. No doubt these have hopes of being our task-masters, and would rejoice at our calamities.

"Look, oh! look, therefore, at your respective states, and anticipate the consequences if these vassals are suffered to enter! It would fail the most fruitful imagination to represent, in a proper light, what anguish, what horror, what distress would spread over the whole! See, oh! see, the dear wives of your bosoms forced from their peaceful habitations, and perhaps used with such indecency that modesty would forbid the description. Behold the fair virgins of your land, whose benevolent souls are now filled with a thousand good wishes and hopes of seeing their *admirers* return home crowned with victory, would not only meet with a doleful disappointment, but also with such insults and abuses that would induce their tender hearts to pray for the shades of death. See your children exposed as vagabonds to all the calamities of this life! Then, oh! then, adieu to all felicity this side of the grave.

"Now all these calamities may be prevented if our God be for us—and who can doubt of this who observes the point in which the wind now blows—if you will only acquit yourselves like men, and with firmness of mind go forth against your enemies, resolving either to return with victory or to die gloriously. Every one that may fall in this dispute will be justly esteemed a *martyr* to liberty, and his name will be had in precious *memory* while the love of freedom remains in the breasts of men. All whom God will favor to see a glorious victory, will return to their respective States with every mark of honor, and be received with joy and gladness of heart by all friends to liberty and lovers of mankind.

"As our present case is singular, I hope, therefore, that the candid will excuse me, if I now conclude with an uncommon address, in substance principally extracted from the writings of the servants of God in the Old Testament; though, at the same time, it is freely acknowledged that I am not possessed of any similar power either of blessing or cursing.

"1. Blessed be that man who is possessed of a true love of liberty; and let all the people say, *Amen*.

"2. Blessed be that man who is a friend to the common rights of mankind; and let all the people say, *Amen*.

"3. Blessed be that man who is a friend to the United States of America: and let all the people say, *Amen*.

"4. Blessed be that man who will use his utmost endeavor to oppose the tyranny of Great Britain, and to vanquish all her forces invading North America; and let all the people say, *Amen*.

"5. Blessed be that man who is resolved never to submit to Great Britain; and let all the people say, *Amen*.

"6. Blessed be that man who in the present dispute esteems not his life too good to fall a sacrifice in defence of his country: let his posterity, if any he has, be blessed with riches, honor, virtue, and true religion; and let all the people say, *Amen*.

"Now, on the other hand, as far as is consistent with the

Holy Scriptures, let all these blessings be turned into curses to him who deserts the noble cause in which we are engaged and turns his back to the enemy before he receives proper orders to retreat; and let all the people say, *Amen.*

"Let him be abhorred by all the United States of America.

"Let faintness of heart and fear never forsake him on earth.

"Let him be a *magor missabile*, a terror to himself and all around him.

"Let him be accursed in his outgoing, and cursed in his incoming; cursed in lying down, and cursed in uprising; cursed in basket and cursed in store.

"Let him be cursed in all his *connections*, till his *wretched* head with dishonor is laid low in the dust; and let all the soldiers say, *Amen.*

"And may the God of all grace, in whom we live, enable us, in defence of our country, to acquit ourselves like men, to his honor and praise. *Amen* and *Amen.*"

SIR RHYS AP THOMAS.

THE character of the family to which Rhys ap Thomas belonged, and his own services rendered in behalf of the Earl of Richmond against Richard the Third, form a remarkable and exceedingly interesting episode in Welsh history. We have concluded to give the account in full, as we find it in the Sketches of Wales, and its scenery, by *Thomas Roscoe, Esq.* London: Henry G. Bohn, York Street, Covent Garden, 1854; pp. 235—256.

The overthrow of Richard the Third and the accession of Henry (Tudor) the Seventh to the throne, formed a turning point in the history of England. In the preceding civil wars it was estimated that between 50,000 and 60,000 persons had been slain. The country had been distracted, improvement checked and the island impoverished.

Among the first acts of Henry was to put an end to the civil strife by marrying Elizabeth, daughter of Edward the Fourth; and thus blended the Houses of York and Lancaster. He greatly advanced the interest of England by encouraging trade and commerce, and abridging the power of the Pope. In his reign was commenced that opposition to papacy, which resulted finally in the permanent establishment of the Protestant religion in England, under the reign of his successors of the Tudor line.

No one who reads Mr. Roscoe's account of the services of Rhys ap Thomas, can suppose that had it not been for his bravery at the head of 2,000 Welsh horse, the field of Bosworth would ever have been won by Richmond, or Henry the Seventh; an event which neither common historians nor the imagination of Shakspeare have done justice.

Henry V. of England, or, as he was called in his youth, Harry of Monmouth, had finished a brilliant career of military achievements at the Castle of Vincennes, in France, and the sceptre of Britain passed from the hands of one of its bravest and most vigorous princes into those of his baby successor. The imbecility of the child was followed by the incapacity of the man; and the reign of Henry VI. gave rise to that ferocious civil contest, known best by the name of the War of the White and Red Roses. It was in the wild mountains of Wales that the White Rose, the emblem of the House of York, first budded, and afterwards became the signal of victory in the sanguinary and well-fought fields of St. Albans, Northampton. Mortimer's Cross, and on the plains of Towton.

At this time, Gruffydd ap Nicholas (whose descendants became at a subsequent period the lords of Abermarlais, in Carmarthenshire) exercised great power and influence in the southern division of the Principality. Ambitious, turbulent, and crafty, he was well-fitted to play a conspicuous part in the stirring times in which he lived. Too choleric to be long at peace with his powerful neighbors, he was alternately engaged in deadly feuds with the leaders and adherents of both the contending parties that disturbed the empire. Consistent and unremitting only in his hatred to the English, he permitted his retainers to commit continual depredations upon the possessions of the Lords Marchers, and to pillage their lands. The injury thus inflicted upon the English borders was too great and frequent to pass unnoticed, and in one of those occasional pauses in this age of civil strife—the quietness of exhaustion rather than the repose of peace—Gruffydd was cited before the king's court, to answer for his violence and contumacy, and Lord Whitney and other commissioners were sent into Wales to investigate his conduct. Gruffydd, who had heard of the commission, but was not fully informed of its objects, laid his plans with the craftiness, and executed them with the boldness, peculiar to his character. He contrived to dissipate any fears which the commissioners might have entertained from his formidable powers, by meeting them on their entry into Carmarthenshire, himself meanly dressed, and accompanied only by four or five attendants "raggiedlie attired," and as miserably mounted. Right glad was Lord Whitney to find the truculent Welshman, as he thought, then in his power, and not a little astonished was he also to hear him, with apparent affability and confidence, offer his services to conduct the commissioners to Carmarthen, the place of their destination. The party moved forward in high glee, each speculating with secret satisfaction upon his success, and conversing with that ease and volubility which belongs naturally to persons so well content with themselves.

Their road followed the windings of the Bran as far as the little town of Llandovery, near which that river unites with the Gwydderig in its confluence with the Towey. On the western bank, situate on a rocky eminence, the castle looked over the whole extent of the romantic vale of the Bran. The united waters of these celebrated streams formed then, as now, that majestic river which is the glory of this part of the Principality. The English lord, and the commissioners in their official array, followed by the humble Welshman, with his tattered attendants, crossed the river by the fine stone bridge a little below the town, and pushed forward in a brisk trot towards the princely mansion of Abermarlais.

The thick woods that lined the shores of the Towey completely hid the towers of the castle from the view of the approaching party. A graceful curving of the road, however, brought them unexpectedly to the foot of the gentle eminence on which it stood. Gruffydd, turning to the surprised commissioners, and pointing to the open postern, pressed them with a smile to enter and refresh themselves, and leading the way across the drawbridge, ushered the party into the spacious court-yard. The wily Welshman was received with demonstrations of the most profound respect by his son Thomas, at the head of a troop of a hundred horsemen, handsomely dressed and gallantly mounted, and the astonished commissioners looked upon an array that began to open their eyes to the power and consequence of their companion.

It was not Gruffydd's design that the commissioners should see too much at once, especially as he had observed that the English lord betrayed some degree of surprise and alarm at the number and excellent appointments of his son's armed retinue; and, therefore, after having well refreshed themselves, the whole party, including the horsemen, defiled from the castle at a round pace, in seeming confidence and cordiality.

"A goodly country this," said Lord Whitney to his companion, "and easily defended, with your mountain passes and these stout yeomen."

"My lord will at least perceive," said Gruffydd, "that I am willing to do him honour, whatever may be the object of his visit to these parts."

Gruffydd had placed a peculiar emphasis upon the word *object*, which at first startled the commissioner, and he remained thoughtful for a considerable time. As the party wound round a long and sinuous defile, which skirted the rocky ridge that in this place beetles above the very shores of the Towey, giving such a picturesque character to the scene, the ancient fortress of Dynevor, not far from the town of Llandilo Fawr, then the stronghold of one of the sons of Gruffydd, suddenly broke upon their view. It was at a considerable distance from the road where it was first discovered by the leading horsemen. The castle stood on the most bold and precipitous eminence of this ridge, overlooking the course of the river, and commanding a view of the open country, and of every approach towards its walls. The party emerged from the defile, and ascended the easy winding road that had been formed on the eastern side of the fortress. Two strong towers of different architecture flanked the spacious courtyard at the northern and southern angles; the latter, standing immediately over a tremendous precipice, was used as the castle *donjon* in these barbarous times, and gave a fearful presage of the secret doom of many a poor wretch who had been its inhabitant. The area was surrounded by high massy walls of great thickness, and was sufficiently ample for the martial exercises of the garrison. Owen, the son of Gruffydd, received the commissioners with great hospitality, at the head of a chosen body of two hundred horsemen under arms, and conducted them into the banqueting-hall of the castle. Owen played the part of the host with admirable skill, and by his address contrived to draw from his guests the secret of the commission, and to assure himself that to secure his father was the great object of their journey. Gruffydd and his sons concealed their discovery from the commissioners, and to prevent all suspicion, treated them with renewed hospitality and attention.

The whole party now pursued their way, increased as it was into a formidable company by the two sons of Gruffydd with their mountain retainers. The road hitherto had run along the base of that mountainous ridge which lines the northern side of the Towey, almost from Llandovery to Carmarthen, until it reaches that bright open plain, where the Gwilli forms its junction with that river, giving its significant title to the little village of Abergwilli. The party had scarcely debouched into the plain, before it was met by a splendid body-guard of five hundred "tall men" on foot, handsomely dressed, and well armed and accoutred, under the command of the elder son of Gruffydd.

Thus magnificently attended, the commissioners entered Carmarthen, then the capital of South Wales, and were conducted with the greatest ceremony to the sumptuous lodgings that had been prepared for them. Gruffydd now excused his further presence upon the commissioners, and committed to his sons the care of seeing to their accommodation, and of attending upon them to the banquet that was prepared in the Guild Hall of the town.

Lord Whitney was not displeased to escape the keen observation of his companion, and finding himself now more at ease, privately sent for the mayor and sheriffs, and, opening to them the commission with which he was charged by the king, demanded their assistance to arrest Gruffydd, which it was agreed should be done on the following morning. The banquet was now prepared, and the commissioners were escorted with much pomp by the sons of Gruffydd, attended by their men-at-arms, to the hall. The tables had been arranged along the centre of the floor, and according to the architecture of these times, a row of pillars, with grotesque, fanciful carvings separated the upper end of the room, which was slightly elevated, and which was usually set apart for the most distinguished guests. To a seat purposely placed here, and splendidly hung with cloth of gold, Owen conducted Lord Whitney, and took his station immediately on his right. On each side of this elevated part of the spacious hall, galleries had been raised, in which were placed the ancient bards of that land of minstrelsy. The guests betook themselves with right good will to dispense the cheer which had been sumptuously provided, according to the profuse hospitality which then prevailed. Owen plied his noble guest during supper, with those sweet-spiced liquors which formed no inconsiderable part of the domestic expense of the nobles, the mixture of which was an art derived principally from the French, and was greatly esteemed by our ancestors in the fourteenth and fifteenth centuries.

> "There was eke wexing many a spice
> As clowe, gilofre, and licorice,
> Gingibir, and grean de Paris,
> Canell at setewale of pris,
> And many a spice delitable
> To eaten whan men rise fro table."

Ypocras and garhiofilac, as being the most prized at this period, with other "delicate and precious drinks," were lavishly distributed on this occasion, and served not a little to produce in the English commissioners a state of convivial carelessness and hilarity. Owen was prepared to take advantage of this, and observing that Lord Whitney had put the commission into the open sleeve of his cloak, he contrived to abstract it from thence unnoticed, and to place it securely in his own pocket. Then turning to Lord Whitney, with great significance, "Methinks our noble guest," he said, "should *lose* for awhile the weighty matters of state, that have doubtless brought him to these rude parts, and do the honor to this festive greeting which our country's customs require. Hither, boy," beckoning to his attendant, "bring our family's hirlas, and see that it lack not of that precious liquor which thy art has taught thee so delicately to prepare."

In a few minutes the attendant returned, bearing the ample hirlas, or drinking horn—usually filled and emptied at a draught at great festive assemblies, which was at once the pledge of fidelity and the expression of personal hospitality. The hirlas which the Welshman presented to the English lord in this case, was of large dimensions and graceful contour, finely polished and richly inlaid with plates of solid silver, chased with the family names and device, and to which was pendent a massy chain of the same precious metal. Lord Whitney knew the custom to which his host alluded, and being too well satisfied with himself to oppose his humour, he drained the contents of the horn with evident satisfaction.

Owen now gave a sign to his favorite bard, Tudor Aled, whose fingers had for some time been gliding rapidly, though silently, over the strings of his harp, which was already placed to do honor to his own and his country's fame.

"Minstrel," said Owen, "thou art wont to enliven our festivals with thy instrument, which I know thou boasted of; prepare now thy happiest strain, such as is suited to this high occasion, and let our noble guest hear what melody thy practised hand can call forth from that harp of thine."

The bard waited not for further parley. He comprehended his patron's meaning, and after sweeping with flying fingers across the diapason of his instrument, as if to instruct his ear in the echoes he meant to awaken, he dashed at once into that bold festive song of the princely poet of his country.

"Fill the HIRLAS HORN, my boy,
Nor let the tuneful lips be dry
    That warble Owen's praise:
Whose walls with warlike spoils are hung,
And open wide his gates are flung
    In Cambria's peaceful days.
By Owen's arm the valiant bled;
From Owen's arm the coward fled
    Aghast with wild affright;
Let then those haughty lords beware
How Owen's just revenge they dare,
    And tremble at his sight."

The guests were all hushed into breathless silence when the bard ceased; and as he gently put aside his harp, whose wild peculiar tones were still lingering in dying cadence within the spacious hall, he exhibited that striking and almost prophetic character which belonged to his order, in its best days, before the cruel massacre of Bangor, when the Welsh bards animated their country's warriors to the fight, or sung their victories. His rich mantle of blue cloth, thickly embroidered with small figures in gold of the raven, his patron's crest, and lined with the fur of the beaver, an animal then not uncommon in the Principality, was fastened at the right shoulder by a massy clasp of polished gold; his vest or tunic was of azure silk, exposing the form of his ample chest as it expanded with the enthusiastic efforts of his minstrelsy; while encircling his neck, a broad gold chain of twisted links, the gift of his patron, had hung gracefully vibrating during the rapid motion of his fingers as they passed along the instrument. The venerable bard arose when his song was finished, and as he leaned upon his "harp so fair," he seemed in the majestic outline and rich illumination of his figure, to stand like the very type of his perished race, invested with the grey antiquity of ages.

"Tall was his form, and thin and spare,
And white as snow his beard and hair;
Back from his brow his white locks flow,
And the high open forehead show;
O'er his pale cheek rich roses fly,
And more than youth illumes his eye."

Lord Whitney was by this time in that enviable state of mental obscuration, from the strong potations that his wily neighbour had pressed upon him, that though he was sensible of a multitude of ideas floating like atoms through his brain, he was incapable of reducing them to any palpable shape or figure; or else, perhaps, he would not have failed to have noticed the singular coincidence of the minstrel's song, with the name and circumstances of his apparently friendly and hospitable host. A flowing wassail cup of rich pyment concluded the entertainment of the evening, and the commissioners were conducted to their lodgings, in a state of happy forgetfulness of the object of their journey, to sleep away the effects of their boisterous revelry.

Owen communicated to his father the success of his plan, but Gruffydd abated nothing of his formal courtesy and attention to the commissioners. He sent his sons in the morning with a numerous retinue to attend them to the Guild Hall, the scene of the night's festivity, where they met the mayor and sheriffs of the borough. Lord Whitney chuckled at the thought of having the redoubtable Welshman so completely in his power, and summoned Gruffydd to attend. He forthwith appeared splendidly dressed, and was immediately arrested by the officers of the court. He made no show of resistance, but with an assumed air of great respect, requested that the proceedings against him might be conducted according to the forms of law, and that the commission, under which he was attached, might be publicly read, alleging that he could not otherwise consider himself bound to submit to the authority of the commissioners.

Lord Whitney readily assented to his request; but upon putting his hand into the sleeve of his cloak, discovered, for the first time, the loss of his commission. Consternation was visible on his countenance, and an inquiry was immediately whispered round amongst the commissioners' attendants for the missing document.

Gruffydd surveyed the party for some time with secret satisfaction, but in complacent silence.

"Methinks, Lord Whitney," he said at last, casting a scrutinizing glance upon the commissioners, "if he comes here by the king's grace as he says, must have valued his commission too highly, lightly to have committed it to the safe keeping of that ruffle, or carelessly to have lost it. Look, my lord, to your piebald coat or your silk hood, you may have placed it there, perhaps, to be nearer your memory." Then starting with fury, clapping his hat hastily upon his head, and turning to his friends and followers—"What!" he said, "have we cozeners and cheaters come hither to abuse the king's majesty's power, and to disquiet his true-hearted subjects, and the good citizens of this our loyal town?" Looking at the commissioners, afterward, with a bitter frown—

"By the mass," said he, "before the next day come to an end, I will hang up all your bodies for traitors and impostors." And immediately ordered his men-at-arms to seize and carry them to prison.

The commissioners were panic struck, and entreated for their lives; which Gruffydd at last granted on condition that Lord Whitney should put on his livery coat of blue, and be bound by an oath to go up to the king, acknowledge his own offences, and justify the Welshman's proceedings. The terrified commissioner, to preserve his life, consented, and faithfully fulfilled his oath.

Gruffydd, continuing his depredations upon the Lords Marchers, was again cited before the king's court, and on failing to attend was convicted of felony. This determined him to break with the House of Lancaster, and to declare for the Duke of York. He joined the Earl of March, the duke's son, with eight hundred men, well armed and appointed, and was slain in the bloody field of Mortimer's Cross, after he had lived long enough to know that victory had declared on the side of the White Rose.

Gruffydd was succeeded in his power and possessions by his eldest son Thomas, who inherited the courage of his father, but in connection with a mildness of disposition and an elegance of manners, rarely united in those cruel times of civil warfare. To avoid intermixing in the contests of the rival houses, he withdrew to the accomplished court of the duke of Burgundy, in whose services he enrolled himself. Here he fell in love with the duke's niece, and to avoid the consequence of his indiscreet attachment, he returned to his native land.

Thomas ap Gruffydd was famous for his boldness and skill in the tilt and tourney, and in single combat. After his return from Burgundy he had several encounters of this latter kind, particularly with Henry ap Gwilym, of Court Henry, in the vale of the Towey, who repeatedly challenged him, and was as constantly vanquished. A quarrel with William, the proud earl of Pembroke, brought upon him another adversary, whose adventures are attended with some humorous circumstances, which, as they tend to illustrate the character of the times, are here related. The earl's quarrel was taken up by one Tuberville, a notable swash buckler of that day, "one that would fight on anie slight occasion, not much heeding the cause." Tuberville sent his defiance to Thomas ap Gruffyd by one of the earl's retainers.

"Go, tell the knave," said he, "that if he will not accept my challenge, I will ferret him out of his cunnie berrie, the Castle of Abermarlais." Thomas received this message very jocosely. "By my faith," said he, "if thy master is in such haste to be killed, I would that he should choose some other person to undertake the office of executioner."

This reply very much provoked the challenger, and in a rage he set out for Abermarlais, and entering the gate, the first person whom he encountered was Thomas ap Gruffydd himself sitting at his ease, dressed in a plain grey frock gown, whom he took for the porter.

"Tell me, fellow," said Tuberville, "is thy master Thomas ap Gruffydd, within?"—"Sir," answered Thomas, "he is at no great distance; if thou wouldst have aught with him, I will bear thy commands."

"Then tell him," said he, "that here is one Tuberville would fain speak with him." Thomas hearing his name, and, observing the fury he was in, could scarcely refrain from laughing in his face. But restraining himself, he said he would acquaint his master; and on going into his room sent two or three of his servants to call him in. Tuberville no sooner saw Thomas ap Gruffydd than, without making any apology for the mistake he had committed, he taxed him roundly for his contempt to so great a person as the earl of Pembroke.

"In good time, sir," said Thomas, "is not my lord of Pembroke of sufficient courage to undertake his own quarrels without the aid of such a swasher as thyself?"

"Yes, certainly," replied Tuberville, "but thou art too much beneath his place and dignity, and he has left thy chastisement to me."

"Well, then," said Thomas, in excellent humour, "if thou wouldst even have it so, where would it please thee that thou shouldst have me to school?"—"Where thou wilt, or dar'st," replied Tuberville.

"Thou comest here with harsh compliments," observed Thomas; "I am not ignorant, however, that as the acceptor of thy challenge, both time, place, and weapons, are in my choice; but I ween that it is not the fashion for scholars to appoint where their masters shall correct them." After this parley, Thomas fixed on Herefordshire as the scene of combat. Here the champions met accordingly; when, at the first pass, Thomas unhorsed his adversary, and cast him to the ground, and by the fall broke his back.

The amusement of men of gentle blood, as they were somewhat strangely called in this rude age, when not actually engaged in civil strife, seemed to be in fierce personal encounters. The next engagement of this kind was in Merionethshire, with David Gough, when Thomas ap Gruffydd killed his antagonist. Having afterwards thrown himself on the ground to rest, without his armour, he was treacherously run through the body by one of his enemy's retainers.

Thomas ap Gruffydd's two elder sons, Morgan and David, became, immediately on their father's decease, warm partisans, on opposite sides, of the two rival houses of York and Lancaster,—and both perished in that murderous warfare.

The inheritance now descended to Rhys ap Thomas, whose first act when he came into possession of the estate, was to put an end to the feuds which had subsisted between the family of Court Henry and his own, by a marriage alliance with Eva, the daughter and heiress of Henry ap Gwilym of that House. By this judicious measure, he added to his possessions a property not much inferior to his own original patrimony. His establishment and hospitality were in every respect suitable to his immense wealth, and displayed the magnificence of a prince, rather than that of a private gentleman. He acquired unbounded popularity, and by degrees very formidable power, by re-establishing the games and institutions of his country on different parts of his estates in Carmarthenshire and Pembrokeshire, and by training the young men to the use of all kinds of arms, under the guise of sham fights and military spectacles.

But to return to more historical details. The fatal battle of Tewkesbury was fought on the third of May, 1471, and by its decisive character seemed to put an end for the present to the hopes of the House of Lancaster. Queen Margaret, whose sagacity and courage had been the guide and stay of her party, was a prisoner in the Tower, and the young prince of Wales, her son, had been inhumanly butchered before the face of the Plantagenet king, for having given a reply worthy of the spirit and magnanimity of his mother. Twelve pitched battles had been fought during this sanguinary contest of the White and Red Roses. In these battles, and on the scaffold, above sixty princes of the royal families, above one-half of the nobles and principal gentlemen, and above one hundred thousand of the common people of England, had lost their lives. The bloody and luxurious reign of Edward IV. was terminated almost prematurely by a death brought on by dissipation and mental remorse; and that of his successor, Richard the Third, was ushered in by a tragedy of the most dismal and savage character, when the two young princes, the children of the late king, were barbarously murdered in the Tower, to make way for Gloucester's unjust and violent assumption of the crown.

The defection of the duke of Buckingham from the cause of Richard the Third had once more raised the hopes of the House of Lancaster, when it became of great consequence to gain the adherence of so powerful a chieftain as Rhys ap Thomas, especially as he held the command of the western coast of Wales and the surrounding district. The king, suspicious of the fidelity of his subjects, sent his commissioners to Rhys, amongst others, to exact an oath of fidelity, which, though somewhat offended at the jealousy manifested by Richard in its requirement, he took without hesitation.

"I would have the king to know," said Rhys to the commissioners, "that such suspicions on the part of princes, might read, to some of fickle minds and unstable thoughts, evil lessons against themselves; for myself, I protest to his majesty that whoever, ill-affected to the state, shall dare to land in these parts of Wales where I have any command, must resolve with himself to make his entrance and irruption over my body."

Not far from the little town of Llandilo Vawr, at the eastern extremity of a fine lake, stood the Abbey of Talley, a name which it derived from its locality.* Its abbot was a zealous partisan of the Earl of Richmond, and the intimate friend of Rhys. Plotting, wily, and persevering, he sought to gain him over to the cause of the Tudor, by alarming his fears at the

* Tal y Llychau, the head of the lakes.

suspicious and sanguinary character of Richard; insinuating at the same time that the visit of the commissioners was an indication that he had already become an object of the tyrant's jealousy and hatred. He succeeded after some time in creating distrust and apprehension in the mind of Rhys, and by the application of that subtle casuistry in which the pious churchmen of those days were eminently skilled, he silenced his scruples as to his oath and his declaration of loyalty.* The abbot avowed his attachment, and that of his neighbour, the bishop of St. David's, to the interest of the House of Lancaster, and he was not long in obtaining from Rhys assurances of support in the same cause.

It was rather more than eleven years after the decisive battle of Tewkesbury, when Henry, Earl of Richmond, afterwards Henry VII. of England, landed at Milford Haven, with a small band of French auxiliaries, to make a desperate, and, as it should then seem, with such inadequate means, a fruitless effort to dethrone the tyrant of York, and to seize for himself the sceptre and crown of Britain. Rhys ap Thomas no sooner heard of the arrival of the French fleet in the bay, than, true to his promise, he ordered the beacon-fires to be lighted on all the neighbouring hills, as the preconcerted signal of the event, and hastened himself, with a noble band of chosen followers well mounted and armed, to greet him. The rendezvous of the partisans of the House of Lancaster was at Shrewsbury, whither Rhys repaired with a select body of two thousand horse, chosen from the flower of his attendants. The armies of the contending parties marched to meet each other, and the important day was fast approaching which should lay for ever one of the contending factions in the dust. It was Sunday morning when Richard moved his long array through the streets of Leicester, to the sound of martial music, with the kingly crown upon his head, and pitched the tents of his disciplined troops, in the evening of the same day, on the field of Bosworth. Richmond was already in the field, and so nearly encamped to his enemy that many of the disaffected in the tyrant's army came over, and joined him in the darkness of the night. The gathering hosts had mustered by early dawn at their appointed posts. The war-cry of the conflicting Roses was once more raised on the peaceful plains of merry England; and a fearful contest, such as when men fight for a crown and kingdom, marked the progress of that fatal day.

Richard, in the heat of the battle, made a desperate plunge

* A popular tradition in the neighbourhood asserts, that Rhys satisfied his conscience by remaining under a small bridge while the Earl of Richmond passed over. This was doubtless one of the expedients suggested by the worthy abbot.

at the Earl of Richmond; Brandon and Cheyne, and many a high-born gentleman, fell before the shock of his fierce encounter. Nothing could resist the fury of his onslaught. He had nearly reached the spot where Richmond stood, when Rhys saw the peril which the Earl's life was in, and mounting his favorite charger, Grey Fetterlocks, which he always reserved for great emergencies, with Sir William Stanley, flew to his rescue. The gallant Welshman encountered the king hand to hand, and after a desperate struggle, slew him.

Richmond was hailed king on the field of battle by his victorious army, and Stanley placed the crown of England on his brow. It was in the calm evening twilight of that tumultuous day when Rhys, Stanley, and the king met together in the tent of the fallen tyrant.

"You have both done bravely, my gallant friends," said the king, "this well-fought field is yours. This day will heal, I trust, the distractions of this unhappy country. Rise, Sir Rhys ap Thomas," he said to the kneeling warrior, "the honor of knighthood is justly thine; and hereafter, in token of this day's service, and the life that I owe to thy valor, I shall call thee Father Rhys." The two knights divided the spoil of the tyrant's tent.

Sir Rhys ap Thomas maintained the fame of his high character in all the bitter conflicts of the reign of Henry VII. He was created a Knight Banneret, loaded with honors, and had conferred upon him the government of Wales. He attended his sovereign in the expedition to France, and took part with the besieging army at Boulogne. When peace was concluded with Louis XI., that artful monarch sent a pension of two hundred marks to Sir Rhys, as he had done to most of Henry's counsellors. Sir Rhys, considering it only in the shape of a bribe, indignantly spurned the offer. "Tell thy master," said he to the messenger, "that if he intends by this to relieve my wants, he has sent too little; but if he proposes to corrupt my mind or stagger my fidelity, his kingdom would not be enough."

The reign of Henry VII., though comparatively peaceful, gave rise to two extraordinary impostures, in the pretensions of Lambert Simnel and Perkin Warbeck to the crown of England. In the severe conflicts of Stoke and Blackheath, which were the consequence, Sir Rhys bore a distinguished part. In the first, the eager valor of the Welsh hero had nearly cost him his life; for, pressing forward before his men in an encounter with one of the Irish commanders, he was beset by several of the enemy, and only rescued from destruction by the timely aid of the Earl of Shrewsbury, who flew to his assistance. After the battle the king, who had been informed of his narrow escape, addressed him jocularly—"How now, Father Rhys, how likest thou the entertainment here? Whether is it better, eating leeks in Wales, or shamrocks among the Irish." "Both certainly, but coarse fare," replied Rhys; "yet either would seem a feast with such a companion," pointing gratefully to the earl who rescued him.

In the succeeding reign of Henry VIII. he was equally distinguished. He possessed the Justiciaryship of the Principality, and gained great honors at the sieges of Tiruenne and Tournay, where he commanded the light horse. On his return he was invested with the office of Seneschal and Chancellor of the manors of Haverfordwest and Rhos, in Pembrokeshire. The latter days of the old warrior were spent in the peaceful retirement of Carew Castle, amidst the mimic exhibitions of those martial spectacles the sanguinary realities of which had engaged and delighted his active life, and in the pageants and festivities of St. George, the patron saint of the order to which he belonged, which he celebrated with a splendor and magnificence that has become matter of history. In the year 1527, the veteran knight sunk to rest, and the holy fathers of the Priory of Carmarthen chanted "*Requicscat in pace*" over the mortal remains of

SIR RHYS AP THOMAS.

HEROIC DEATHS OF WELSH REGICIDES; OR, OF CROMWELL'S COMMONWEALTH MEN.

We have stated in another part of the Appendix that a number of Welshmen and their immediate descendants were the supporters and followers of Cromwell, sometimes spelled Crumwell.

At the Restoration, Charles II. was induced to issue a sort of amnesty to the regicides of Charles I., which caused many of them to return to their homes and families. Several of these were subsequently seized, briefly tried, condemned, hanged and quartered, on charges of treason. Among them were Col. John Jones, Revd. Hugh Peters, Genl. Thomas Harrison, and others who were natives of Wales. Genl. Thomas Harrison was born at Nantwech, in Cheshire (the Nantwich of Camden). They all died like Christian heroes. None recanted their high-wrought and holy religious belief, with which they had set out in their efforts to overthrow tyranny and to sustain civil and religious liberty ; promoted, as they believed, by the establishment of the Commonwealth. Genl. Harrison, without abating an iota of his love of civil and religious toleration, disapproved of some of the late acts of the Protector. The behavior of these men who were led to execution at *Charing Cross* was heroic in the extreme. Their Christian hopes and faith enabled them to triumph to the last. If " Socrates died like a philosopher, and Jesus Christ like a God," the regicides died as became the disciples of Jesus Christ and believers in a just God.

General Thomas Harrison, on coming from the Tower of London to Newgate, preparatory to his execution, sent word to his wife that " that day was to be his wedding day."

When chains were put on his feet, he exclaimed " Welcome, welcome," declaring that his Master had worn a crown of thorns, to which these chains were nothing. A woman who had been in his cell to prepare it for his reception, on coming out was asked how the Major General behaved. She said that " never was there so good a man in that place before." He parted cheerfully with his wife, and said he had nothing to leave her but his Bible.

He called out on his way to execution, saying " I go to suffer upon the account of the most glorious cause that ever was in the world." When near the scaffold one of the Royal scoffers called out to him in derision, saying " Where now is your good old cause ?" He, with a cheerful smile, clapped his hand on his breast, and replied, " Here it is, and I am going to seal it with my blood."

He was cut down alive after hanging a short time, when the inhuman executioner ripped his bowels open and cast some of his entrails into the fire before his face. Transported at the barbarity of the executioner, he suddenly and convulsively raised himself up, and gave the brute a blow on the side of his face.—*See* " Howell's State Trials," vol. 5, p. 1236. Also, vol. 7, pp. 166 and 1650.

Rev. Hugh Peters, when he entered Cromwell's service, was a dissenting minister, and his family belonged to Carmarthenshire, Wales. By his wisdom and courage, he was said to have been of the greatest service to the Protector. While in Newgate, preparing for execution, two of the king's chaplains paid him a visit, and gave him to understand that, if he would confess his guilt, repent and recant his principles, he might expect the king's clemency. He flatly refused compliance with their propositions, and immediately dismissed them, treating their overtures with scorn. The only minister he afterwards permitted to see him, was a dissenting clergyman of his own faith.

Cook, another regicide, who was hanged and quartered just before it came to the turn of Peters, was ordered by the Sheriff to have his mangled remains carried before him, that he might gaze upon them. One Turner, a royal butcher, who had cut up or quartered Cook, approached Peters, with his hands and clothing all besmeared and reeking with blood, and tauntingly said to him, "Come, how do you like this, Mr. Peters? How do you like this work?" The brave old Christian Cymro replied in tones worthy of his race and of his faith, "I am not, thank God, terrified at it, you may do your worst."—*See* "State Trials," as above.

Col. John Jones, of Wales, was a brave and distinguished officer in Cromwell's army—an army that never knew defeat. He, in advanced years, with Col Scroop, were both dragged together on a sledge to execution. Scroop was hanged and quartered first. Col. Jones, seeing Col. Scroop's young daughter convulsively weeping for her father, kindly took her by the hand, and soothingly said to her:—"You are weeping for your father; but suppose your father had been made King of France and you were to tarry a little behind, would you weep so? Why, he has gone to reign with the King of kings in everlasting glory." On the day of his execution he grasped a friend by the hand, and said with expressions of tenderness, "Farewell; I could wish thee in the same condition as myself, that thou mightest share with me in my joys."—*See* "State Trials," vol. 5, p. 1286.

All these regicides made public speeches from the scaffold and offered up prayers for the people, and for the king himself. Their addresses breathed a noble spirit of Christian faith, hope, and resignation. They sealed their love of civil and religious liberty with their blood, and never did Christian martyrs suffer more nobly. No wonder the people of England, under the tyranny and misrule of the Stuarts sighed for "THE GOOD OLD DAYS OF QUEEN BESS!"

We envy not the devotion to monarchy which led historians like Hume, Scott, Macaulay, Allison, and others, to plaster over and apologise for the dastardly and cruel conduct of the imbecile Stuarts, while seated on the throne of England.

The profligate Charles the Second could, if he had been disposed, have witnessed the hanging and quartering of those noble Christian patriots from his palace window; and might have put an end to their blood-shed, by simply raising a finger, yet, his royal vengeance knew no satiety, and its last victim was duly slaughtered. Notwithstanding the absence of every spark of true nobility of soul in the bosom of Charles, he failed not to find laudatory defenders among historians both in Scotland and England.

The bigoted, cruel, and imbecile James the First could lead a noble knight, like Sir Walter Raleigh—a man "without fear and without reproach"—from 20 years unjust incarceration to the block, and yet find historical eulogists!

Hume and Scott's inflated panegyrics of the Stuarts, and their defamation of the Tudors, and especially of Elizabeth Tudor, is only equalled by the misrepresentations of Papal historians. We hope that some day their perversion of historical truth will receive the exposure and condemnation it deserves. The distortion, either through ignorance or prejudice, of Welsh ethnology and history, by many authors—and, especially by Hume, Pinkerton, etc.—is as extraordinary as it is manifest.

But we can tell these revilers and perverters of historical truth that, notwithstanding their attacks, sustained as they have been by great intellectual ability, that

> "*Cymru fu Cymru fydd,*"
> "Cambria that was shall ever be."
> "*Tra mor, Tra Brython,*"
> "While exist the sea, the Briton shall be."

On the site at *Charing Cross*, where the regicides were

hanged and quartered, stands the Equestrian Statue of King Charles. The day may arrive when a monument, consecrated to CIVIL AND RELIGIOUS LIBERTY, will rise in its stead; with the names of JOHN HAMPDEN, THOMAS HARRISON, HUGH PETERS, AND JOHN JONES, and the names of OTHER MARTYRS to that glorious cause—THE GREAT CAUSE OF HUMANITY, FOR ALL TIME.

EXPLANATORY NOTES.

THE following occurs in the Dictionary of Dr. OWEN PUGHE.

"Alp, s. m., pl. au (Al) a craggy rock, a precipice; a word common in the mountains of Glamorgan—hence *talp*. *Isodorus*, *Servius*, and *Phylagyrius* say that the word ALPS, in the Gaulish language, signifies mountains; which confirms its Cymbrian origin."

Hence, it is possible, that the *Appenine* mountains of Italy may have been derived from *ap*, of, and *pen*, head—springing from the head mountains of Europe. *Alpen* was, probably, abbreviated into *Alps*.

A tribe of Cymbrians is said to have occupied, anciently, a very deep valley in the north of Italy, which was shaded and shut out by high mountains, which cast their dark shadows over it—hence the term of *Cymerian darkness*.

ISAAC WAYNE, the son of General Anthony Wayne, who, in 1838, resided in Delaware County, Pennsylvania, told a highly respectable Welsh gentleman of this city, that his father's ancestors came to Pennsylvania from Wales.

MADISON and MONROE were of Welsh descent, on the female side of their families. On the male side, Madison was, probably of English descent, and Monroe was supposed to have been of Scotch origin.

We have said that feudalism was not introduced into Welsh polity, until after her union with England; hence, there were no offices of heraldry in which worthless "loafers" could seek reputation in ancestors; which they were too lazy to gain or incapable of earning for themselves. Owing to the long prevalent custom of transmitting or of changing the first and Christian names into surnames, (which was also common in France and especially in Brittany) it would, after a few generations, become measureably impossible to trace genealogies at all. The Welsh idea is, that every man must stand individually responsible for his own acts, and that he can claim no special merit on account of his family progenitors, and neither is he to be condemned for their demerits.

We have referred, in another place, to the doctrines of the Druids.

As their lessons were delivered orally and only preserved among themselves, partially engraven on three-sided sticks (hence called Triads), but little has transpired of a positive nature to show their character.

"Of the lessons thus habitually taught, few specimens are found in ancient authors. Mela. iii., c. 2, has preserved one of them; and says, in Latin, that one of their precepts has become public, namely, that which bids them remember

> "To act bravely in war;
> That souls are immortal;
> And that there is another life after death.

"Diogenes Laertius has presented us with another, in Greek, as follows:—

> "To worship the gods;
> To do no evil;
> And to exercise fortitude.

"Both of these precepts are Triads; and, hence, we may conjecture that such was the *form* of their moral and historical instruction."—*See* Davies' Celtic Researches, pp. 150—151.

Alexander Hugo, in his work on "France, Historical and Monumental," Vol. I., in treating of the *Science and Maxims of the Druids*, among others gives the following:—

> "The world is eternal;
> The soul is immortal;
> The world, if destroyed, it will be by water or fire."

Again:—

> "A father of a family is king in his house."

We give the following maxims from the Bardic Druids:—

> "*Nid Duw ond dim;*
> *Nid dim ond Duw.*"
> "Whatever is God can not be matter;
> Whatever is not matter must be God."

It is probable that the reason they taught their laws and doctrines in Triads, and thus arranged important *truths* in *threes*, was to fix them more indelibly upon the memory of the people, at a time when manuscripts were few and printing unknown.

The Druids in Britain and Gaul, it is said, existed there for more than one thousand years before the birth of Christ. Now as their doctrines, as above proclaimed, were not taught in ancient Greece until the days of Pythagoras, Plato, and Socrates—about 500 years before the Christian era—it is fair to infer that they were derived, in Greece, from the early teachings of the Druids—a most extraordinary race of pagan priesthood.

Alexander Hugo locates the ancient Ligures around and to the west, and north west of Genoa, and the Etruscans, in the valley of the Arno, in Tuscany. This matters little, however, as the latter were, no doubt, also a branch of the Cymry. Mr. Davies, above referred to, states that the Welsh Bardic alphabet and that of the Etruscan were the same.

CAMBRO-AMERICAN ARTISTS

Among these, without wishing to be invidious, we may name Mr. POWELL, the author of De Soto's discovery of the Mississippi, whose family, it is said, came from South Wales. Thomas D. Jones, of this city, the sculptor, and one of the most successful modellers of busts in the United States, is of Welsh parents; he having been born at Remsen, Oneida County, New York. And Thomas Buchanan Read, who came of a Welsh family, settled in Pennsylvania, is considered among the most eminent poetical scene painters in the country.

If space permitted, we could also name several successful musicians, of Welsh origin or descent.

The Rhuddlan Parliament Stone, referred to in another place, is said to be preserved in the cathedral of St. Asaph, North Wales, where it was removed.

Letter of SAMUEL JENKINS, Esq., of Philadelphia, author of "Letters on Welsh History," To the Author of the Address; *Dated February*, 1853.

I received your Letter, the past week. In reference to your inquiries: I presume it would be best to place the notices of distinguished men in proper order, and I propose to do so under the four different heads of *Warriors*, *Statesmen*, *Bards*, and *Divines*. War is an offensive subject; yet, some of the most virtuous of the human race have gained immortal renown by defending their country against oppression.

I shall first proceed to notice Caradog, commonly called Caractacus, son of Bran or Brenus, Prince of Siluria, in South Wales. Of his fame I have no doubt that you are well informed.

Casibellanus, who fought against Cæsar, was king of the Casi, a people living about Herefordshire.

After the first war there did not appear to have been much trouble between the Welsh and the Romans; but, upon the decline of the Roman power, the Cimbric tribes in Wales, and especially the Silures, began to put forth their strength. True it is that Conant, Prince of North Wales, aided his brother-in-law, Maximus, to obtain the empire, towards the close of the fourth century: and, though Maximus failed, Conant held on to Brittany, in France, the emigration to which, from Wales, was large, and imparted new energy to it.

I will begin my notice with some account of the princes of North Wales, the first of whom was Caswallon. He was called Prince of Gwynnedd, which territory comprised a strip of land along the Irish Channel, of about 200 square miles. He was grandson of Cunedda, Prince of Cumberland; and drove the Irish out of the island of Anglesey (or Mona), after they had kept it for 29 years. He reigned 74 years, or until about 443, and died in the beginning of King Arthur's reign. He left his principality to his son, Malgwyn, who was also a man of great energy of character. He was then young, and had several uncles acting in concert with him. His fame as a powerful warrior induced his uncles to place him at the head of affairs.

From that time, till the year 606, there does not appear to have been any man of great note at the head of affairs in North Wales; although Run, the son of Malgwyn, maintained his position.

In the year 603 (or, at farthest, 610), the Saxons under two of their kings, at the instigation of the Pope, through Austin (or St. Augustine), named the Apostle to the Saxons, and other agents, came and destroyed the great seminary of Bangor Iscoed and overran the greater part of the middle of the principality, called at that time Powis; then governed by Brochvael Ysgythrog. They had the further design of destroying the primitive churches in Wales, or to compel them to submit to the Pope's supremacy and accept the dogmas of Popery. But the princes of North and South Wales, uniting with Brochvael, chose Cadvan ab Iago, Prince of North Wales, commander, and defeated the Saxons with terrible slaughter. After the death of this great prince, he was succeeded by his son, Cadwallon, who defeated the Saxons in fourteen pitched battles, besides successfully meeting them in many minor battles and skirmishes; but he was finally overwhelmed by numbers, and killed. He was succeeded by his imbecile son, Cadwallader, who, after some years, turned papist, and ended his days at Rome. His own people, however, were far from being papists. Prince Cadvan was worthy of being ranked with Epaminondes.

The princes of North Wales were a most active and brave set of men.

The most prominent among them appear to have been Llewelyn ab Seisyllt and his son, Griffith. The former was brave, and skilful in war, but disposed to peace. The principality, nnder his government, had twelve years of repose. His son, Griffith, however, was, like Pyrrhus, warlike; and successively defeated Saxons and Danes, including some bodies of Normans; and, turning his arms towards South Wales, defeated the people of that section, in four pitched battles, in the last of which the prince of South Wales was killed.

This contest was fomented by Saxon rulers, who found means to set those of the South against the North.

The princes of South Wales had, in the sixth century, struggled as strongly against Popery, attempted to be fastened upon them by Saxon rulers, as those of North Wales.

These contests between the Welsh and Saxons continued at intervals until Harold, who, being the last Saxon king and claiming to succeed Edward the Confessor, made peace and raised the whole force of England into a grand army to oppose the invasion of William the Norman. This movement, with the treachery of the bishop of Bangor, finished the life and reign of Griffith. His head and the beak of his ship were placed on the Tower of London.

The next distinguished prince of North Wales was Griffith ab Cynan, who ended his reign of 57 years at the age of 82, in 1135, '36, or '37—I quote from memory. Henry the First, of England, and Griffith ab Rhys, Prince of North Wales, died about the same time, or within the space of three years from each other. This prince was succeeded by his son Owen, to whom even his father owed most of his prosperity. Owen stands about the highest of the princes of North Wales, as to military fame. He displayed from youth great military talents. He was over thirty years of age when his father died, and preserved till he was over eighty-nine years the same great martial qualities. He had seventeen sons, all of whom attained the age of manhood, and generally inherited and displayed their father's heroism. His eldest son, Edward, was set aside on account of some deformity in his nose, and he was succeeded by David, a younger brother,who was, after a few years set aside for marrying a sister of Henry the Second, of England ; and his nephew, Llewelyn, the son of the broken-nosed Edward, was chosen prince and, during a reign of 42 years, displayed a degree of valor worthy of his race and of the brave people whom he governed. He married Joan, the amiable daughter of King John.

Both Henry the First and King John granted the Welsh chiefs considerable territories in England, in hopes, thereby, to secure peace on the borders. But there was little hope of that; for I doubt whether there ever was, in the world, a people more intent upon war than the people and princes of North Wales—a small principality which contained, at the outside, at that early period, only about 80,000 to 100,000 souls ; and whose most powerful expeditions amounted to 8,000 men, 6,000 foot and 2,000 horse. It appears, however, to have been one of the most complete military schools in Europe.

Llewelyn, son of Edward (called in Welsh Llewelyn ab Iorwerth, or Llewelyn son of Edward), was succeeded by David ab Llewelyn, who reigned five years and died without issue. Llewelyn ab Griffith, grandson of Llewelyn ab Iorwerth, was chosen prince, and was the last prince previous to that title being transferred by a compromise, under Edward the First, to the heir apparent in the Royal House of England, which occurred in 1283, after Llewelyn was betrayed and slain on the River Wye, Brecknockshire, South Wales.*

* The veneration in which the Welsh people hold the recollection of Prince Llewelyn, down to the present day, is truly remarkable. He succeeded in rallying his brave countrymen in a severe defensive struggle against Edward the First—the Alexander of the Norman line of kings—who strengthened his army by large re-inforcements from France. Llewelyn had defied his power in North Wales, in many a hard-fought battle ; and, during a visit which he paid to South Wales for the purpose of uniting the chiefs in that quarter in support of the war, he suddenly found himself in Radnorshire, with a small force, in the vicinity of a large body of English troops. He was forced to retire westward; having his horses' shoes turned, to evade pursuit, at the small town of Aber Edwy, in Radnorshire. He re-crossed the Wye, and proceeded to near the confluence of a small stream, called the Ivor, with the Wye, where he awaited the drawing of his men together. To guard his position, he posted a portion of them at the chief passage of the Wye, having destroyed the bridge at Builth. His men were flanked by the English, who crossed at another point of the river ; and a scouting party fell upon Llewelyn, whose pursuit had been aided by the reversed tracks

The principality of North Wales after its establishment, in 443, maintained its independence 840 years. Neither the Spartans nor any other people ever excelled the people of that principality, in courage and patriotism, or ability in war.

They, also, had many of the finest poets in Europe.

The last Llewelyn is said to have been the most accomplished of any of the Welsh princes; but he had to contend against Edward the First—the greatest of the English princes, —whose kingdom was, probably, forty times as large as that of Llewelyn's; to say nothing of the mercenary enlistments of Irish, French, and Spaniards, whom he employed as auxiliaries on different occasions.

I shall next proceed to notice the distinguished men of the Silurian tribe, whose territory was the eastern part of South Wales. The first warrior who is best known in history, was Caradog or Caractacus.

After the Romans retired from Britain, there was Vortimer, son of Vortigern (called by the Welsh, Gwrtheyrn), who was a brave prince of high virtue.

After him came Ambrosius and the great king Arthur, who was succeeded by many other chiefs of great fame in Welsh history. But from 606, or thereabouts, the princes of North Wales eclipsed those of the South; yet, when South Wales was tottering to its fall, there were three great princes who manfully sustained it. These were Rhys ab Tewdwr (Tudor) his son Griffith, and his son Rhys. This latter prince was alive in 1188, but I can not tell the year in which he died. It must, however, have occurred soon after, as he commenced his reign in 1136, at the age of twenty. He was the philomen of South Wales. After his time, the princes and chiefs of South Wales and Powis became tributary to the crown of England, and many of them were made barons.

of his horse in the snow, betrayed to them, it was said, by the blacksmith who had changed the shoes.

He was slain by one Francton, who at first did not know him, but returning to despoil his victim, who had lingered alive for a short period, he discovered his real character and proceeded to finish his work, by cutting off his head; which was sent to London.

A few Welshmen, with the aid of a pious old Welsh clergyman, proceeded to bury the body on the spot where he was slain, in a small open space in the woods, near where a high road now passes; and which, to this day, remains destitute of vegetation. And, although about 600 years have clapsed, since he was buried at that lonely place; and, although no stone yet marks the bleak ea th where his last remains crumbled to dust; we doubt whether there is a single Welshman, in the whole Principality, who cannot conduct a stranger to his grave—*Cefn y Bedd*, or *Cefn bedd Llewelyn*—"the Ridge of Llewelyn's grave."

In other parts of the world, such men's tombs have been perpetuated by immense marble columns, or tablets of bronze, or by the erection of sacred temples; yet, none of these have been, or are likely to be, more enduring than the strong national associations with which, and probably for all future time, the Welsh will keep in remembrance the humble grave of the great, good, and brave Prince Llewelyn.—*See* THEOPHILUS JONES' *History of Brecknockshire.*—A. J.

For about 100 years, the princes of North Wales waged almost continual war with England, and the policy of both was to gain over as many of the Welsh chiefs as possible. Strange, that such a petty district should dispute empire with the kings of England, both of the Saxon and Norman lines!

After Wales acknowledged tribute to the crown of England, on having obtained a representative prince in the Royal family, the most noted Welsh warriors were Owen Glendower, in North Wales, and Sir Rhys ap Thomas, in South Wales.

Two gallant men, Col. Morgan and Sir Roger Williams, went over and aided the Dutch, in Holland, to throw off the Spanish yoke.

There have been distinguished Welsh military men of modern times, both in America and in England.

In the wars between England and France were General Sir Thomas Picton, the Marquis of Anglesey, and, I believe, Sir Stapleton Cotton.*

Among the Welsh statesmen we have to notice their first and most ancient and renowned law-giver, Dyfnwal Moelmud, who flourished before the birth of Christ.

Attempts have been made to represent him as a prince of Cornwall; but, at the first period of authentic history, his Institutions were in full force in Wales. To him is ascribed the institution of Trial by Jury, which was practiced in South Wales; as you may learn at the end of the Triads of the social state. The laws of Dyfnwal Moelmud were revised by Bran, the father of Caractacus. The second revision took place under Howel Dda, or Howel the Good, Prince of South Wales, who died in 948, after a reign of about forty years. The general principles of these laws will be seen in the Triads of the social state.

There was a general assemblage of all the learned men, who appointed a committee to revise the laws; among whom was Blegwryd, a most eminent lawyer. The committee consisted of thirteen, the prince having nominated the thirteenth, named Blegwryd, as above stated. He was dean of Llandaff, and eminent for his learning and knowledge of the laws.

Since that period, Welshmen have had few opportunities for the display of statesmanship. I, however, have no doubt but Britain and the world at large would have been benefited had they exercised more influence, and especially in England.

* The Duke of Wellington, on his mother's side, descended from Sir John Trevor, a Welsh baronet, and derived his name of Arthur, through that Welsh family. Afterwards, his mother's family name became changed, by marriage, to Mornington. *See* account of Sir John Trevor, in W. C. TOWNSEND's *Lives of the Judges*. Also, consult the *Lives of the Judges*, by W. WELSBY, Esq. Dr. OWEN PUGHE's *Cambrian Biography*. Also, the *Welsh Biographical Dictionary*, by the Rev. Mr. WILLIAMS, of Llanarvan.—A. J.

Of poets, the most eminent were Taliesin, Merddin, Aneurin, Llywarch Hen, and the wild Merddin, of the fifth and sixth centuries. There were bards in all ages; yet, bardism or poetry, in the twelfth century, shone out in wonderful splendor. Among others, of that period, were Owain, Prince of North Wales (the great warrior) and his son, Howel; and Owen Gyfeiliog, Prince of a part of Powis; and Gwalchmai, an eminent commander under Owen, Prince of North Wales, and also son of the same. Also, David Benfras, in the thirteenth century; Griffith, son of the Ynad Coch; David Williams (also called Davydd ab Gwilym) in the fourteenth century; and Tudor Aled, poet-laureate to Jasper Tudor, uncle to Henry the Seventh; together with great numbers who flourished in the reign of the Tudors, including the reign of Queen Elizabeth Tudor. Among them were Edmund Prys, dean of Merioneth, who composed the psalms of David into verse, in the Welsh language. Afterwards, there was Hugh Morris, the song writer, who died in 1709. Succeeding times produced Sion Rhydderch, David Manuel, Jenkin Thomas, and his sons, John and Nathaniel Jenkins. The former was my great-grand-father. The works of these three poets are to be found among the most choice Welsh secular poetry. Among others were Lewis Morris, the patron of Goronwy Owain. There are, however, many poets in North and South Wales whose names I do not now recollect It would not, however, do to forget the Revd. Goronwy Owain, who ended his days at Williamsburg, Virginia; and who was an Episcopal minister. One of his grandsons was in Congress, from the State of Alabama, a few years since.*

In sacred poetry, the first on the list, in the composition of hymns, was the Rev. William Williams; who was second to none but Watts; and believed by those who know both languages and competent to judge, to be superior to Watts. Mr. Williams was one of the first Calvinistic Methodists.

David Jones, the farmer—who translated all of Watts' psalms and hymns, the divine songs and the cradle hymn, into Welsh verse—also composed a book of poems of his own.

We have also to notice Benjamin Francis, a Baptist minister; and Ann Griffith and Mr. Morgan Rhys (pronounced Rees) a layman; with many others. The Welsh hymnology is

* Thomas Lloyd Jones (known by his bardic name, *Gwenffrwd*), who was born at Holywell, Flintshire, at the age of twenty-two, produced the most splendid poetry in the Welsh language; which must forever challenge the admiration of his people and the world at large, if made accessible. He took two prizes at the Eisteddfod or bardic celebration, at Beaumaris, in 1832; one of which was bestowed by the then Princess Victoria (now Queen of England), her mother, the Duchess of Kent, being present; and the other by Miss Charlotte Williams, the accomplished daughter of the president of the Eisteddfod. He died of fever, near Mobile, at the age of twenty-four, in 1834.—A. J.

equal to that of the English; and we have also in our language all of Watts' compositions, besides those originally written in the Welsh language.

Dr. Owen Pughe translated into Welsh Milton's *Paradise Lost*, which he executed in a scholarly-like manner.

Last, but by no means least, was David Richards, commonly known as *Davydd Ionawr*. He composed a poem called the *Trinity* which in certain particulars, according to my judgment, excels *Paradise Lost;* not so much as a work of genius —although, in that respect, it is of the first order—but throughout the whole work, of upwards of ten thousand lines, there is evinced the most ardent and passionate love of the subject of Revelation and Redemption; the entire poem being based on the soundest principles of theology. I am satisfied, however, that there is nothing in the English language to equal it, except Milton's *Paradise Lost.**

Mr. Richards was astonished in his youth at the truths respecting the Incarnation of Divinity, and his whole production seems to be the result of love and admiration of Divine Grace for its compassion on sinful man. The work is a pouring forth of the passionate love of a soul overwhelmed with a sense of its deepest obligations to its Creator and Redeemer. It is impossible for any Christian to read it without great excitement on the same subject. His episode on Joseph covers forty-five pages, of thirty-eight lines each. The work begins with the Creation and ends with the Final Judgment.

The promise of the Saviour, and the longing of the pious for the coming of the Messiah—the dream of Heli, the father of the Blessed Virgin, and the comfort which he receives in the fact that she was beloved of God—her song which she sung, in company with her harp, to comfort her blessed parent; and, after his death, a song in which she expresses her confidence in the protecting care of God—the Annunciation, by the Angel, of the truth of the Redeemer—the various scenes on the plains of Bethlehem—the Visitation of the wise men—the Cradling in the Manger—the song of Simeon—the ministry of John and that of the Redeemer—the Crucifixion and Resurrection—the Ascension into Heaven—are all portrayed in a masterly and sublime style. Nor are the various visits to the grave, on the auspicious morning of the third day, without the most touching effect on any pious mind. And I had never before seen painted the scenes of the last great drama,

* John Milton was born in London, December 6th, 1608; and was christened as John Mylton. His mother was Sarah Castor, "a lady from Wales," and who was said to have been a woman of incomparable virtue and goodness, and exemplary for her liberality to the poor. His wife, Mary Powell, was a native of Flintshire, Wales. *See* the *Poetical Works of John Milton, with a memoir, etc.*, by JAMES MONTGOMERY. Hartford: S Andrus, 1847.—A. J

proclaimed by the sound of the last trumpet, in such a masterly manner, until I saw this great poem. I had always given the English poets the precedence, but now I am compelled to claim for the Welsh a very exalted position.

True, they may not have produced much in the line of Shakspeare; but we must consider that, up to the year 1700, the population did not much exceed 300,000.

There have been other poetical works, produced by men of genius within a few years. Among these I may mention Dewi Wynn, Dafydd Ddu, R. ab Gwilym Ddu, Eben Fardd, Gwilym Hiraethog, Caledfryn, Ieuan Glan Geirionydd, Rev. John Blackwell, and Thomas Edwards (Twm o'r Nant), who was called "the Shakspeare of Wales." These, however, I know only by reputation, not having seen the works.*

* Maria James was a poor Welsh girl and self-educated poetess, of a high order. She emigrated to the United States while a child seven or eight years old, then unable to speak any other language than her native Welsh. The first English words she learned, she said, were acquired on board of the ship, in which she came over; and which were "Look out" and "Get out of the way."

After her arrival in the United States, having attained the proper age, she served in some respectable families as nurse; and subsequently became a domestic or help in the family of Mrs. Freeborn Garretson, who was sister of the late Chancellor Livingston and of the late Hon. Edward Livingston. The husband of Mrs. G. was the well-known and eminent minister of the Methodist Episcopal Church.

The poems written by Maria James were collected into a volume and edited by the Rev. Alonzo Potter, D. D., the bishop of the Protestant Episcopal Diocese of Pennsylvania; to which he added an introduction and a brief sketch of her own humble life, well written by herself. These poems were published by John Taylor, of New York, in 1839; and attracted attention for the high order of poetical genius and religious sentiment they exhibited. They were entitled "*Wales, and other Poems,*" and contained 170 pages.

The work abounds in many beautiful passages, which would do credit to some of the best English versification.

Her opening stanzas to Wales breathes a pure and touching affection for the land of her birth. We here give a few verses from it, taken at random:—

Beyond the dark blue sea,
  Beyond the path of storms,
Where wave with wave, in converse loud,
  Uprear their forms—

Westward on Britain's isle,
  The rocky cliffs are seen,
With cities fair, and ruin'd towers,
  And meadows green.

But cities fair, or towers,
  Are not so dear to me
As one lone cot that stood beside
  A spreading tree.

Though dim on memory's page
  The recollections rise,
As backward, through the vale of years
  I cast my eyes;

Yet well I mind the fields
  Where best I lov'd to roam,
Or meet my father when at night
    Returning home.

* * * * *

Altogether, I must say, that there is in the Welsh people a peculiar genius. That, however, which has interested my mind above all other traits in their character, is the fact that they

And well I mind the flowers,
In gay profusion spread
O'er hill and dale, and how I deck'd
My garden bed.

For there the summer sun
Unfolds the cowslip-bell,
And there the cuckoo's voice is heard
In shady dell.

There Snowden lifts his head
To greet the rising day,
Whose latest glories linger round
The summits gray.

There sleep her sons of fame;
There rest her bards of yore:
And shall the Cambrian lyre
Awake no more?

* * * * *

I heard Jehovah's praise,
In Cymru's native tongue,
And hung upon those artless strains—
In rapture hung.

* * * * *

'Twas in that tongue that first
I heard the voice of prayer,
Beseeching Heaven to take us all
Beneath its care.

* * * * *

Land of my fathers! ne'er
Shall I forget thy name—
Oh! ne'er, while in this bosom glows
One transient flame!

We, also, give her Ode entire, written for the Fourth of July, 1833; just after the subsidence of the Nullification Tariff excitement, and which breathes a devoted spirit of patriotism and love for our Union.

I see that banner proudly wave—
Yes, proudly waving yet,
Not a stripe is torn from the broad array—
Not a single star is set;
And the eagle, with unruffled plume,
Is soaring aloft in the welkin dome.

Not a leaf is pluck'd from the branch he bears
From his grasp not an arrow has flown;
The mist that obstructed his vision is past,
And the murmur of discord is gone;
For he sees, with a glance over mountain and plain,
The union unbroken, from Georgia to Maine.

Far southward, in that sunny clime,
Where bright magnolias bloom,
And the orange with the lime tree vies
In shedding rich perfume,
A sound was heard, like the ocean's roar,
As its surges break on the rocky shore.

never attempted to fetter the mind in its researches after truth; having been the only people who had discernment enough to see the excellence of the Gospel, they were enabled to learn that it could not injure society.

The government was in the hands of the people, for both male and female possessed the elective franchise; accordingly, "the sovereign people" did not wish to put manacles on their own limbs. They gave certain stipends to the Druids, because they wanted to prevent disorder and riot without the intervention of severe penal laws. They had rather prevent crime by the fear of the criminal sinking into the pig, or something still more degrading, than to have them commit murder and other crimes; and be obliged to hang them. Yet, if any system was proposed which had a like tendency to benefit public morals, the Welsh would look upon it impartially; and treat the teachers according to the merits of the system they taught. In these respects the Gospel may be supposed to have been acceptable to the Welsh; but as the worst punishment of sinners under the Druidical religion was only temporary, the poets and princes continued to be attached to it for many centuries, as well as many of the people

* * * * * *

I would never have troubled my head about history, so far as to write anything about it, had it not been that others had

Was it the voice of the tempest loud,
As it fell'd some lofty tree,
Or a sudden flash from a passing cloud
Of heaven's artillery?
But it died away, and the sound of doves
Is heard again in the scented groves.

The links are all united still,
That form the golden chain—
And peace and plenty smile around,
Throughout the wide domain:—
How feeble is language—how cold is the lay—
Compared with the joy of this festival day—
To see that banner waving yet—
Aye, waving proud and high—
No rent in all its ample folds;
No stain of crimson dye:
And the eagle spreads his pinions fair,
And mounts aloft in the fields of air.

Her work also contains beautiful lines, written in memory of the late Rev. Mr. Garretson; with some lines written on seeing a bust of the late Hon. Edward Livingston, which indicated:—

"A soul, transfused through every part.
That chained the sense and won the heart."

The Exile: supposed to be addressed by a Polish lady to the Picture of her Son—is a piece of uncommon merit. Her pieces on *Pride*, and the *Broom*, are quite original, and touched with piquant pleasantry.—A. J.

entirely overlooked one of the brightest pages in the history of man.*

I have not as yet said anything about Welsh ministers of the Gospel. There are a great many whose names are recorded in the early history of Wales, together with those of a great many eminent teachers. Among the distinguished teachers were Cadwig the Wise and St. David; for David himself, although a primitive Christian bishop, was never a Roman Catholic. He was both a popular preacher and afterwards a teacher. The Welsh, in primitive times, had from twelve to fifteen colleges, some of them large; having had at times from 1000 to 2000 students. They were destroyed by the Papist, in the dark ages. They, however, could not suppress the national desire for education; and private teaching was continued and independent anti-papal feelings cherished until the House of the Tudors came to the throne, and the Reformation or primitive Protestantism of Wales, as it were, became permanently established over all England; greatly assisted, it is true, by other favorable causes.

I will proceed to give the names of a few of the most eminent ministers of Wales in modern times. And, as many of them belonged to the Established Protestant Church, I will begin with them; first, however, premising that Bishops Reginald Peacock and Davies, in the fourteenth century, were Welshmen.

After the Reformation there were Bishops Parry and Morgan, of St Asaph's; Rudd, of St. David's; Lloyd, of St. Asaph's; and Williams, who was Archbishop of York; besides many other good and eminent bishops.†

* The English people, containing a large element of Welsh origin have, with the Americans, done much to spread civilization abroad.

In whatever part of the globe their flags and their language have gone, men of Wales or of Welsh descent have gone with them; and have aided to extend their ancient principles of civil and religious liberty, embraced in the laws of the two countries.

They have also supplied many useful missionaries to distant lands. Among others, we may be permitted to mention S. Wells Williams, who was born in Utica, New York, and was of Welsh descent.

He has spent many years in China, where he has learnt to write and to speak the language, and conducts a large printing establishment in Chinese. He also acquired a familiar knowledge of Japanese, which he speaks and writes. He acted as interpreter to Commodore Perry, in negotiating the treaty with the Japanese, and rendered very important services.

The Rev. Mr. Roberts, a very successful missionary to China, of Welsh descent, visited the rebel camp at an early period; and was well received. He distributed religious books among them, and subsequently visited the United States.

We could name many other devoted missionaries, of the same origin or descent, if our limits permitted.—A. J.

† Richard Baxter, the author of the *Call to the Unconverted* and of *Saints' Everlasting Rest*, was born in Montgomeryshire, North Wales; and, it is said, that he did not speak any English until he was eighteen years old —See *Life of*

Among the Baptist ministers of Wales were John Perry and Vasavor Powell; and the following three who were born of the same mother, viz.: Abel Morgan, Enoch Morgan, and Benjamin Griffith; the latter having sprung from a second marriage (the first husband having died young); the first, or Abel, was settled in Philadelphia; and the second, Enoch, at Duck Creek, Delaware. Abel Morgan, the son of Enoch Morgan, settled at Middleton, New Jersey. Enoch Francis and Benjamin Francis, father and son, were also eminent preachers. There was also the Rev. David Jones, chaplain to the American armies during the Revolutionary war and also during the war of 1812; the Rev. Thomas Evans and his son, Caleb Evans; and his grand-son, Hugh Evans; the latter of whom was Principal of the Bristol Academy; and his son, Caleb Evans, D. D., who succeeded him in the same Institution. There were ten ministers of this family connexion; about eight from Enoch Francis: there were Timothy Thomas, and his brothers, Joshua and Zachariah; and, of their descendants, ten or twelve more.

In the family connexion of the Morgans and Griffiths, abovementioned, there have been about thirty ministers and preachers, in the old and new world. They commenced with a deacon of Rhydadian church, but only about ten or twelve were Baptist ministers. Some belonged to other independent Protestant churches.

I am the fifth descendant of Morgan Rhydderch in a regular line of descent from his oldest son, who remained in Wales when Abel and Enoch came to America.

The name of Christmas Evans is well known; and there was a multitude of other ministers, many of whom were men of great ability.

William Williams, Esq., of Cardigan, a Justice of the Peace and President of the Court of Quarter Sessions, was a man of great ability and distinction.

It is vain to attempt to enumerate all who deserve to be mentioned. Extended notices of those who were distinguished as Independent ministers would, alone, fill volumes. Among them, however, we may name Walter Cradoc, Lewis Rees, Jenkin Jones, David Lloyd, Owen Davies, Williams of Wern, Benjamin Evans, Lewis Jones, Jenkin Thomas, Roger Williams; and hundreds of others, in every age, since the Reformation.

The Calvinistic Methodists commenced with five able men,

Baxter, in Welsh, by the AMERICAN TRACT SOCIETY; and also IEUAN GLAN GEIRIONYDD's "*Gwladgarwr*," *Bywgraffiad Baxter*.

Some English authors have incorrectly placed the birth of Baxter at Rowton, Shropshire, close on the borders of Montgomeryshire, but all contemporary Welsh authors place his birth in Wales, and give details of his early youth.—A. J.

viz.: Howell Harris, Daniel Rowland, Peter Williams, Howell Davies, and William Williams. The latter was the Watts of Wales.

Since that period, they have had hundreds of most able ministers. Among them, I may name David Morris and his son, Ebenezer; David Jones of Langan; John Elias, and Jones of Edeyrn; David Rees, and David Evans; with hundreds of others.

This body of Methodists were blessed in the zeal and ability of its first founders, almost beyond any other sect; having commenced with five such eminent men. Daniel Rowland was one of the ablest ministers and eloquent men of modern times.*

I have not space to enumerate the ministers of these sects. The Independents have had so many able ministers and teachers in academies that, to pretend to give an account even of the most prominent among them, would prove too great a task.

In fact Wales has been, of all countries, the most blessed with able and faithful Gospel ministers.

Great numbers have settled in England and America, while no country has supplied Wales.

I could, if time permitted, greatly extend these remarks; but I must close.

I have written these few lines in great haste, as I am exceedingly pressed with business matters.

I am, very respectfully, yours, etc.,

SAMUEL JENKINS.

CYMBRIC OR WELSH NAMES.

THE etymology of the names of persons and of things go very far to distinguish the ethnological differences of a people, and form a very curious subject of inquiry.

It may be premised that the names of *Wales* and the *Welsh* are of Saxon origin, and of comparatively modern date.

The Welsh have always called themselves *Cymru* or *Cymry*, Romanised into *Cambria* or *Cambrians*. We have no doubt that this has been the generic name of the race, from a very remote period of antiquity. The Romans changed *Gal* into *Gaul:* the Welsh sound *u* as *e*; hence they pronounced the Romanised word Gaul, as *Gael.* The Saxons, as was their

* Rowland Hill was said to have come of a Welsh family.—A. J.

wont, substituted *W* for *G*; hence, as the people of Cambria were esteemed to be analogous to the Gauls, they called their country *Waels* or Wales, and its people *Waelsh* or Welsh; and these names have continued to the present time.—*See* Dr PUGHE's Welsh Dictionary.

We have stated that the Irish and Welsh languages widely differed. To prove this, it is only necessary to give the respective alphabets of both dialects.

"General Velancy, in his essay on the antiquity of this language, has given a full comparative vocabulary of Irish and Punic-Maltese words, with their significations; and also a comparative declension of a noun for each tongue, of the same meaning; and he is decidedly of opinion that it has been derived through the Phœnic or Carthaginian from the Phœnician, and therefore concluded that the Irish language is a Punic-Celtic compound. This language, probably, also prevailed at a remote period, in Spain; from whence a large portion of the population of the western and southern portions of Ireland were supposed to have come, as the followers of King Milesus, hence called Milesians.

The Irish alphabet commences with the letter B, having L and C next, with A about the middle; but, for the sake of uniformity, we submit the letters in the usual rotation. "This alphabet was supplied by a gentleman of Baltimore, who taught the Irish in Ireland, by the approbation of the present Queen of England."—See *Pantography or Parsigraphy, relating to the Science of Letters*, by BENAJAH J. ANTRIM, pp. 122. Philadelphia. 1847.

IRISH ALPHABET.

A, B, C, D, E, F, G, I, L, M, N, O, P, R, S, T, U.

WELSH ALPHABET, IN ITS ESTABLISHED ORDER.

A, B, C, CH, D, DD, E, F, FF, G, NG, H, I, L, LL, M, N, O, P, PH, RH, R, S, T, TH, U, W, Y.

THE FOLLOWING IS THE PHŒNICIAN ALPHABET.

A, B, G, D, E, V, CH, I, C, L, M, N, O, K, R, S, T.

It will thus be seen that the Irish alphabet has but seventeen letters and no double consonants, while the Welsh alphabet contains twenty-eight letters and eight double consonants, and in this particular resembles the ancient Greek, which has twenty-four letters, four of which are equivalent to double consonants. It would be difficult to imagine a similarity of languages, where the alphabets so widely differed. It would appear that, at a very remote period, there existed other dialects in Ireland of which but little is known.

The Phœnician alphabet, above, contains eighteen letters and only one double consonant.

It is this alphabet, says General Velancy, which the present Irish alphabet most resembles. The signs adopted by each, to represent their letters, of course widely differed. The Welsh alphabetical signs, in a number of cases, closely resembled those of the ancient Greek, but at an early period they adopted the Roman letters.

Alexander Hugo, previously referred to, has given a vocabulary of words in Scotch, Gaelic, Cambrian, Cornwall, Armorican, and Breton, in France; to prove that the language of each was essentially the same.*

All the northern and eastern part of Ireland, probably, at one time, used the Gaelic language; the primitive population prior to the Milesian invasion having, it is supposed, been composed mainly of the same race, as that in a good part of Scotland.

It is a curious fact, as shown by Dr Owen Pughe, that the Welsh language contains a large number of words which not only resemble those of the ancient Greek, but also those of the Hebrew. This he has proven by a long list of words taken from each, and with their orthography and signification in their originals, compared with the Welsh.

The Hebrew ancient and modern alphabets, contain twenty-two letters, and no less than seven of each are duplicates.

WELSH NAMES OF PERSONS.

Previous to the introduction of Christianity, Welsh names were derived from geographical positions, or the character of the pursuits, or the physical circumstances of the individual. Thus Morgan was derived from *Mor*, sea, and *gan*, near or by. If Morgan had a son he would be called *Gwyn*, white. He would then be known as Gwyn ap or ab Morgan, the *p* and *b* being commutable letters.

After the introduction of Christianity, if Gwyn had a son he would call him John or Mathew, and who would then be called John or Mathew ap or ab Gwyn; if John or Mathew had a son he would be called Phillip or Daniel ap or ab John (or Jones) or Mathew—Jones being derived from John.

Williams comes from the conversion of William into a surname in the same manner; hence, the Welsh names are readily recognised whenever spoken; because their Christian names have been converted as a general thing into surnames without any prefix, such as Mc, Van, etc., or termination of son.

A large number of Welsh names are found in the eastern

*See Mémoires de L'Académie Celtiques, V. vols., Paris, 1809-10; W. F. Edwards. Recherches les Tongues Celtiques, Paris, 1844.

sections of Ireland, many of whose ancestors went over with the forces of the Earl of Pembroke, surnamed Strongbow, in the time of Henry the Second. Among the officers of the Earl were Maurice Fitzgerald and Robert Fitzstephens, both sons of Lady Nesta, a daughter of Gryffith, a Prince of South Wales. The first was her son by Gerald, governor of Pembroke Castle, and the second by Maurice, constable of the Castle of Cardigan.* The descendants of these two persons are found in Ireland to the present day. The ancestors of Father Mathew and Bishop Hughes went over, it is said, about the same time. At a more recent period the family of Oliver Goldsmith, the author, went over; whose mother was the daughter of the Rev. Oliver Jones, after whom he was named.†

It is needless to add that the northern and eastern parts of Ireland contain a large number of Scotch names.

Welsh names have, in many cases, experienced a singular transformation in the following manner. Ap Richard has, by dropping the *a* and joining the *p* to Richard, been changed into Pritchard; Ap Rice into Price; Ap Howell into Powell; Ap Hughe into Pughe; Ab Owen, by dropping the *a* and joining the *b* to Owen, has been rendered into Bowen; Ab Rees into Breese; Ab Evan into Bevan; etc.

WELSH NAMES OF SCRIPTURAL ORIGIN.

Adam or Adams, (*also Scotch*)
Abel,
Daniels,
David,
Davis, / Davies, / Davy, } *Corruptions of* David.
Ellis or Elias,

* *See* KNIGHT's History of England—reign of Henry II.

† Goldsmith's grandfather, the Rev. Oliver Jones, was a Protestant clergyman, as was also Charles Goldsmith, his father. The former belonged to or sprung from a Welsh family, and probably went to Ireland after the establishment of Protestantism in England. He was established at the church of Elphin, and was master of a school at that place. Oliver Goldsmith was born November 9, 1728.

Though named after his maternal grand-father he claimed affinity or connexion with Oliver Cromwell, and he also claimed kindred with General Wolfe.—See *The Miscellaneous Works of* OLIVER GOLDSMITH, *a New Edition, with an Account of his Life and Writings.* London; 1820, 4 vols.

The writer, when on a visit to London, in 1841, through a brief 'City Item' he read in a London morning paper, found JOSEPH GOLDSMITH, a nephew of Oliver Goldsmith, living in a narrow, dirty street, near Westminster Abbey, at seventy years of age, in extreme indigence. He was employed, up a pair of stairs, in an old building, teaching small children at twopence each, per week. We conversed with him about his uncle, whom he distinctly recollected, and described his relationship in such a way as to leave no doubt of his identity. We wrote a note to Charles Mathews, the manager of the Covent Garden-theatre, suggesting the propriety of getting up a play for his benefit. This failing, we published an account of his case, in April or May, 1841, in the London *Herald*, and appealed to public charity in his behalf, which had the effect of relieving him. We went to see him afterwards, and found him better off. Among others who had called to see him was a wealthy lady, in her carriage, named Goldsmith, who gave him several pounds in money.

Enoch,	Paul,
Isaacs,	Phillips.
James,	Peters,
John or Jones,	Samuels,
Luke,	Stevens, or Stephens,
Marks,	Thomas,
Mathews,	Zachariah.

NAMES OF CYMBRIAN ORIGIN OR ETYMOLOGY, CHIEFLY FOUND IN WALES.

Aetius, from *edyf*, thread; the general who defeated Attila, on the plains of Chalons, 451.

Adden, from *add*, impulse, and *en*, source of life.

Allain, *al*, high, and *ain*, a breathing principle.

Allen, from *al*, high, and *en*, source of life.

Anstruther, from *struth*, foaming, uproarious.

Arthur, from *arth*, a bear.

Alwyn, bright, fair.

Anwyl, dear.

Balch, proud.

Baulch, from Balch.

Bevan, from *ab* Evan.

Bowen, from *ab* Owen.

Breese, from *ab* Rees.

Brice, from *ab* Rice.

Brochvael, from *broch*, a tumult, and *mael*, traffic.

Brock, from *Broch*.

Cadvarch, from *cad*, war, and *march* a horse.

Cadvan, from *cad*, destruction, and *man*, a place: *v* being commutable with *m*.

Cadwallader, from *cad*, war, and *gwaladr*, a ruler.

Cadwallon from *cad*, to destroy, and *gwallon*, errors; *g* being silent.

Caswallon, from *cas* and *gwallon*.

Cass, from *cas*, to insulate, cover, separate.

Carew, from *carw*, a hart, a stag.

Cemmaes or Kemes, from *cefn*, open, and *maes*, a field.

Clymer or Clymwr, a knot tier.

Cocke, from *coch*, red.

Conway, from *cynwy*, head water, name of a town.

Corwin, from *coryn*, a dwarf.

Camden, from *cam*, a bend, a crook, and *din*, to surround a border.

Crew, a shout.

Castor, from *cas*, insulated, and *tor*, a prominence, a pinnacle.

Dewi, to will.

Dervel, from *der*, stubborn, and *fel*, like.

Diana, from *Di* and *anaf*, blameless; Goddess of beauty.

Dyfnwal, well-founded.

Darwin, from *derwen*, an oak tree; from whence, it is said, *Derwydd* or Druid was derived-a Welsh name for theologian. The Druids worshipped amidst the primitive oaks of the forest. On plains they erected vast stone altars, while among mountains they spoke to the people from those raised up by God.

Dryden, from *dry*, economy, skill, and *en*, source of life.
Dragon, a leader; hence, Pendragon, a head leader, commander-in-chief.
Duylin, from *du*, black, dark, or muddy, and *llyn*, a pool or lake; the Welsh name for Dublin, Ireland, referring probably to its ancient topography; hence also, the Welsh name for Liverpool was derived from *llyn*, a pool and *llifer*, (pronounced *liver*) to flux, to flow; or, *llynllifer*, a flowing pool, Anglicised into Liverpool. A small crane once inhabited the Mersey, called in English liver; hence, the Coat of Arms of the city is a small crane called in Welsh, *llifraid*. London is called in Welsh, *Llundain*.
Ednyfed, refined, pure.
Edwin, pale, fading.
Elwyn, bright, clear.
Emlyn, from *em*, a gem, and *llyn*, a lake.
Edmond, from Edmunds.
Edwards, from Edward.
Emrys, from *brys*, haste.
Esyllt, fair.
Ethan, from *eth*, progress, motion, and *an*, a principle.
Evan, from *ieuan*, young.
Evrog, the founder of York.
Ferris, steel, fire steel (*also a Scotch name*).
Far, from *fer*, dense, solid.
Floyd } *Corruptions of* Lloyd
Floy }
Foulke.
Francis, from *franc*, free.
Frances, from Francis.
Gwilym, William.
Glyn or Glen, a valley.
Gorwith, from *gorwydd*, a summit, top.
Griffith, from *gruff* (pronounced *greef*), fierce, terrible.
Griffin, *corruption of* Griffith.
Gwin, from *gwyn*, white.
Gething or Giddings, ugly.
Gwynnett, from *Gwynedd*, the name for North Wales.
Ham, a cause or circumstance.
Hall or Hale, from *hall*, salt, brine, or saline hence, *Halle*, in Germany, which is said to have been an old Wendish town.
Hughes, from *Hu*, a term for deity, demi-god, or god-like
Herbert, or Hubert from *hybert*, expert.
Hill, an augmentation, nimble.
Huber, apt to please.
Howell, from *hywel*, easily seen, visible.
Han, out of.
Hen, old, ancient.
Hob, aptness to rise.
Hoe, respite, quiet.
Hely, a hunter, to call together
Humphrey, yeoman, a domestic place.
Hamdden, leisure, spare-time, respite.
Huelin or Hewlit, a gleam, sunshine (*found also in France*).
Holl, all, the whole (*the root of Holland*).
Harris or Harries, from Harry
Heli, brine, salt-liquor.
Iorwerth, Edward.
Ivor, from *mor*, the sea.
Hun, a selfish principle, one's self.
Jenkins, from *ieuan* and *kin*.
Kenyon, from *ceinion*, beauteous.
Kirk and Quirk, from *cyrch*, to assemble.

Lee, from *lli*, a current or stream.

Llewelyn, from *llew*, a lion, *gelyn*, an enemy—a lion enemy.

Llenfer, light.

Lewis, from *llew*, a lion [*Ludwig in German and Louis in French*]

Lloyd, from *llwyd*, gray.

Lyman, from *lli*, a stream, and *man*, a space, a place.

Llyn, a lake or pool.

Lewin or Llwyn, spontaneous motion.

Mars or March, God of war (*same as in Latin*)

Morgan, from *mor*, sea, and *gan*, near or by.

Morris or Maurice, from *mor*, sea, and *ys*, water.

Morse, *a corruption of Morris*.

Malgwyn, from *mal*, like, and *gwyn*, white.

Madox or Madog, from *mad*, good; son of Owain Gwynedd. Welsh history contains accounts of Madog having made several voyages of discovery, in one of which he is believed to have discovered America. On his return he fitted out a larger expedition, and sailed for the new world in about 1190, from a small port within 3 miles of Holyhead, called *Tre-Fadog*, Island of Anglesey, it being his last or final voyage, and was never heard of afterwards. Had he returned Columbus might have been anticipated in his discovery

Merin, that drops or trickles.

Meredith, from *meredydd*.

Mygar, from *mygr*, majestic, grand, glorious.

Merchyr, from *march*, trade.

Mowrth, from *maw*, to expand to conquer.

Merl, a little horse.

Miles, from *milwr*, a soldier.

Neptune, from *nawf*, to swim, or navigate, and *Neivion*, God of the seas [*as in Latin*]

Nye, from *ny*, universal.

Oliver, from *oli*, to proceed. lastly, and *fer*, dense, solid

Owen, from *o-wain*, unsheathed

Panton or Pennon: epithets for the Deity.

Price, from *ap* Prys or Rhys.

Penn, head.

Pennant, from *pen*, head, and *nant*, a ravine.

Pritchard, from ap Richard.

Powell, from *ap* Howell.

Parry or Perry, from *ap* Harry or Henry.

Patrick, from *pa-trig*, to reside among us.

Penryn, a promontory or headland.

Penry, from *ap* Henry.

Porther, from *porthi*, aid.

Rees, from *rhys*, ardency, signally.

Reynolds, from *rhinallt*, a fox.

Rice, from *Rhys*.

Richards, from Richard.

Rogers, *in French*, Rogé.

Roberts, from Robert.

Roderick, from Welsh of Rhodri.

Rowland, an old Welsh name, from *rholyn*, a roll or roller

Sawyer, *sawyr*, savor, taste.

Tennant, from *ten*, stretched out, and *nant*, a ravine.

Tudor, from *Tywder* [*same as* Theodore]

Tor, a prominence.

Trevor or Treva, a place of resort.

Vaughan, from *bychan*, little.
Walter, from *gwallter* or *gwalther*, long-haired, or *gwalltwr*, a hair merchant.
Watkins, from *gwadu*, to refuse, to deny.
Wadkyn, from Watkins.
Wayne, from *gwain*, a scabbard
Williams or William, from *gwylio*, to watch.
Wyt or Wit, from *wyt*, art, thou art.
Wynn, from *gwyn*, white
Wys or Wyse, from *g-wys*, a summon.
Wyth, state of being, extended identity.
Wight, from *wy*, water, *ynys*, an island; *hence*, Isle of Wight.
Wyngan, from *Wyn*, white, and *can*, pure, bright.
Wyngate, *wyn* and *gate* [*same as English*].
Wynifred, from *gwyn*, blessed and *ffrwd*, a stream.

A great many more names might be added. Some few contained in the list are extinct in Wales at the present day, probably having been superseded in some cases by their conversion into Christian surnames. Many of them still exist in Scotland, France, England, Holland, and Germany; or their derivatives.

We hazard nothing in saying that much over half the names borne by the people of England are of Ancient British origin or derivation; which proves that neither the invasion of the Romans, Saxons, or Normans, extirpated the aborigines of the Island or materially lessened the previous population. To this day, the animus, the vitality (if we may so call it, of what should be termed the *Brito*-Saxon instead of Anglo-Saxon, and still less Anglo-Norman, the latter from British Armorica) has been derived from the ancient inhabitants of the Island, and from whom the Welsh have descended, mostly unmixed, to the present day.

The etymology of more than three-fourths of the names in Scotland are of Cymbrian origin, and probably nearly one-half of those of France. Cymbrian names are also found in the north of Italy; about the Pyrenees, also in Switzerland, Holland, and on the Rhine and Elbe; proving the extent of country the Cymbrian tribes overspread, in their exodus west from the Caucasus.

We shall proceed to give the etymology of names found in Scotland, France, and Holland, premising however, that many of the names given cannot be strictly confined to either locality, as they may be met with in any of the places named as well as in England and Wales. Many of those given under the Scotch head are so common in England as to have become long nationalised.

There are in England and Scotland many names which terminate in *well* or *ton*, and which are believed to have been derived from *wel* or *wall*, to behold, to see now at last, and *ton*, a coat, an outer-coating, a finish, or *ton*, to break out, a wave, or *ton*, an accent. The first would seem to be the one adopted.

There are a great many English names which commence with a Cymbric word or words and end in *ton*, so of *wel* or *wall*. Some, however, have supposed *ton* to mean town, and *wel*, good to do, and to be of foreign origin. This is a point, however, that admits of doubt. *Son* is said to be of Danish and Norwegian origin, as John*son*, the son of John. The termination *ham* is supposed by some to be of Saxon origin, and to come of *hamlet*, a small village: yet we have the Welsh word *ham*, which means a cause or circumstance.

To discuss these matters further would exceed our limits. We could fill volumes with Scotch, English, Welsh, French, Hollandic, and many German names of Cymbrian etymology.

In the progress of the Cymry races through the country now known as parts of Germany, watered by the Elbe and the Rhine, both the names of places and of men would in Cymbrian become mingled with words in the language of the Teutonic races, who succeeded them in the subsequent possession of the country; hence, many German or Teutonic words and those of Welsh have the same meaning, while the Wendish language may be considered a Welsh tongue, corrupted by Sclavonic and Teutonic admixture.

SCOTCH NAMES OF CYMBRIAN OR WELSH ETYMOLOGY.

Albright, from *albrys*, extreme haste, cross-bow.
Alason, centre or middle part.
Alan, *same as Welsh*.
Ayres, from *air*, clear, bright.
Brai or Bray, one that is over, an omenous bird.
Brag, a spouting out.
Bas, a shallow or shoal.
Bradus, to fracture or to break
Bache or Bach, a hook, a grappling iron.
Bath, from *badd* (pronounced *bath*) a bath, a bathing place.
Baldwin, from *bal*, high, and *dwyn*, to carry; also continental.
Bragaw, from *bragawth*, to spring from, a spouting out.
Bell, a tumult, a war.
Bela or Belan, from *bell*.
Bryan or Bryant, from *bryan*, a hill, (*also Welsh*)
Buchanan, from *bychan*, little, and *an*, element or principle
Boyd, to sustain, to nourish, aliment.
Brice, from *bry*, elevated.
Bruce from *bry*, (proncd. *bru*)
Bard, from *bardd*, a bard.
Cass, *same as in Welsh*.
Campbell, from *camp* and *bell*.
Cam, bent, crooked.
Camp or Kemp, a circle, a feat, a game, also the prize obtained at the games. The Welsh had 24 games or qualifications that might be called their course of education, divided into three classes:—10 manly 10 of youth, and 4 inferior qualifications.

Car, or Ker, near, close at hand
Craig, a rock (*the same in Welsh.*)
Cram, an incrustation.
Comins or Cummins, from *com*, a curve, a round, and *in*, to pervade.
Collen or Cullen, a twig, a hazel tree.
Clay, from *clai*, earth or marl.
Cabell, from *ca*, to keep, to defend, and *bel*, war.
Colin, from *colyn*, a pivot, a sting.
Cannon, a song, a rule.
Cornell, an angle, a corner.
Corbell, fair, distant.
Cothial, from *cothi*, to cast, to throw.
Clap, a mass, a round piece.
Church, from *cyrch*, a centre, a goal, gathering towards a centre.
Connel, a tail, a termination.
Don, distinct, to spread out, uppermost, name of a Scotch river.
Dun, united or accordant.
Dunbar, from *dun* and *bar*; a bar, a shaft of a spear; also *bar*, a summit.
Dor, what encloses, a limit.
Dwyer, a little star.
Duncan, from *dun*, and *can*, clear, brightness.
Ferris, steel (*same as in Welsh*)
Fer, *ffer*, dense, solid, fixed, strong metal.
Ffar, that extends out or over.
Farlan, from *ffar*, and *llan*; a clear place for gathering together, village, church, or place of meeting, (pronounced in Welsh, *klan*); hence probably the Scotch term, clan or clans.
Gallt, energy, power.
Gordon, a covering, a shield.
Galbraith, from *gal*, a plain, and *braith*, diversified.
Geofrey, *Latinized from* Gruffydd.
Glasgow, from *glas*, blue or greenish blue, and *go*, progress towards, approach—probably from its proximity to the sea.
Greeve, from *gruf*, *greef*.
Gore, from *gor*, what is superior.
Good or Goode, from *god*, to depart, to swerve, to change
Godardd, soft flowing.
Grey or Gray, from *gre*, sevral together, a company.
Gronyn, a single grain, a particle.
Gross, from *gro*, pebbles, coarse gravel [*also Gallic*]
Grew, spread or laid even.
Gower, a small field, an inclosure.
Gowyn, rather white, whitish.
Gran, sharp, projecting ledge.
Glenn, a valley.
Gough, from *gof*, an artist, metallurgist, a smith.
Gregor, from *greg*, to make a noise, and *or*, outer, extreme, a border.
Greg, from *greg*.
Grennell or Grinell, from *gren* a porcelain vessel, and *ell*, divide or divided [*also Gallic*]
Hall, salt, saline, brackish, or briney.
Hamil, from *ham*, a cause, and *ill*, motion, progress, (*also Welsh*); hence, Hamil-ton.
Hay or Hays, from *hai*, quick, impulsive.
Haw or Haws, from *haw*, full
Heber, locomotion, about, &c. [*Welsh, and Hollandic*]
Hog, to whet, to sharpen

Holly, from *holi*, to investigate, to question.

Hopper or Hooper, from *hopr*, to acquire, to swallow up.

Hogan, a youthful person of either sex, a minor.

Howe, ease, quiet, languor

Houghton, probably from *hotan*, a wood, a cap; or *hotyn*, closing round, a cap.

Hollis, from *hollus*, whole, complete.

Holt, from *Hollt*, a rent, a cleft or rift

Hume or Home (the *o* being mutable with *u*) from *Hu* and *me*, an agent

Hubble, from *hobel*, what hops or starts, a bird, a fowl.

Hubbard, from *Hu* and *bar*.

Hugh, from *Hu*, God-like.

Ion, a source of being [*also Gallic*]

Irwin, from *Ir*, that is pure, and *wyn*, white.

Kilt, from *Celt* or *Kelt*.

Llary, a mild placid man, easy to please.

Lee, *same as the Welsh name*.

Lees, *same as* Lee *in Welsh*.

Law, from *llaw*, a hand; with adjective means upper-hand

Kirk, from *cyrch*, a centre, a goal, tending to a centre, a mark, invasion.

Maury, from Maurice [*Morris*]

Murray, or Moray, *a corruption of* Maury.

Medel, a reaper.

Marian, a level, a strand [*also Gallic*]

Man, epithet for a hand, a place

Main, slender, fine.

Maull or Maul, from *mawl*, a tribute, gratitude, worship

Mur, firm, fixed.

Munroe or Monroe, from *mon*, that is separated, and *rhos*, a rose; *in other words* a plucked rose.

More or Moore, from *mor*, sea; also applied to land partially overflown with water, sea-like.

Non or Nun, a stream, brook.

Nol, to fetch or to bring.

Nye, from *ny* [see *Welsh list*]

Osian, from *Osi*, to offer, to do, to attempt, and *an*, an element, a principle.

Osgood, from *os*, which tends to increase, and *good*.

Or or Orr, from *or*, extreme, a border.

Pell, an extreme limit, a verge

Pall, a spreading, incompact.

Plaid, that parts or divides—such as stripes.

Ray or Rae, from *rhae*, constraint, a battle, a chain.

Rhan, a part, a share.

Rall, from *rhal*, a specific division or part.

Ranne, from *rhanu*, to part, to share [*also Gallic*]

Reynolds, *same as Welsh*.

Rive or Reeves, from *rhyf*, [pronounced *ruv* or *riv*.]

Ross, from *rhos*, a rose; or *rhos*, a meadow.

Sawyer, savor, taste.

Tennant, from *ten*, spread out and *nant*, a ravine.

Tartan, from *tar*, a pervading principle, and *tan*, to cover or spread out. The Tartan plaids or stripes were said to have been derived from the garments worn by an Order of Druids; hence, while they served for a covering, they by their stripes, represented a principle of Druidical religion.

Voy, from *ffoi*, to retreat, to escape.

GALLIC NAMES OF WELSH OR CYMBRIAN ETYMOLOGY.

Allain, *the same etymology as Welsh.* Allain, Duke of Brittany, in France, accompanied William the Norman with Breton troops when he invaded England, and had lands assigned him in that country.
Alger, from *al*, high, and *ger*, utterance, cry.
Arpent, a French measure for land similar to an acre, from *ar*, surface, and *pen*, head.
Arian, pert, quick, witty.
Bacon (commutation of Macon) from *bacon*, berries.
Bar, the top, the summit; hence De Bar.
Bara or Baras, bread.
Bant, high place.
Bannon, one that is exalted.
Banc, a platform a table.
Ban, prominence, high, lofty.
Balch, prominent, towering, superb.
Bache, *same as the Scotch.*
Balau, to spring out.
Barran or Baron, open, in view
Barrow, from *barynw*, topmost, upmost, superior, elevated
Bertha or Berthe, from *berth*, fair, pleasant, rich, perfection, beauty.
Beri, a kite, a glede.
Beriau, short yoke.
Bernard, from *ber*, a spear or pike, and *nar*, forward.
Berthoud, from *berthud*, fair land.
Blys, a desire, to long after.
Byron, from *byr*, short, and *on*, to rise up, that is over, superior, or beyond [*a Brittany name.*]
Bryan or Bryant, *same as the Scotch etymology.*
Burr, from *byr*, short.
Calon, the heart
Canrobert, from *can*, white or bright, and Robert; *in other words* Robert White.
Colbert, a sharp hillock, a peak.
Colon, a point or peak.
Cusan, a salute.
Curas or Cuiras, from *cuiras*, a cuirass.
Canad, a bleaching.
Canaster, from *canaster*, a hundred joinings.
Causten, from *cau*, to enclose to hedge in, and *tyn*, fast, tight.
Caen, a covering, a coat.
Chateaubriand, from *chateau*, a mansion, and *bryan*, a hill; *literally*, a house on a hill or hill-house; hence the residence of Madame Sevigne, near Nantz, was called Chateau Buron or Byron.
De Foe or De Voe, from *ffo*, to retreat, flee, to seek refuge.
Duran or Durand, from *Duw*, God, and *rhan*, a share, a portion.
Drouyn, from *dry*, conspicuous, and *yn*, state of being.
Duryn, a beak or bill.
Dugan, from *dygan*, to chant or sing.
Dubys, from *Duw*, God, and *bys*, a finger.
Ducho, above, over, upward.
Duchan, a lampoon.
Edward, *Edourd.*
Foi, from *ffoi*, a retreat.
Fer and Ferris, *see* Scotch and Welsh.
François, from Francis.
Gerry or Gari, from *geri*, choler or bile.

Garrow, from *garw*, rough.
Garwin, from *gerwin*, rough, severe.
Garrone, name of a river, from *garw*, rough.
Gwathma, from *gwath*, shore or ledge, and *ma*, identified, produced.
Hayne, from *hain*, to pervade, to spread through, to influence, &c.
Huber or Hubert, *see* etymology of Scotch and Welsh names.
Hutan, a name for a bird
Hugo, from *Hu* and *go*, approach towards.
Halpen, from *hal* and *pen*.
Huger, from *Hu* and *ger*, at hand, to utter a cry.
Hugens, from *Hu*, and *gan*, near or by.
Hugueno or Huguenot, from *Hu*, God-like, and *gweno* (pronounced *gueno*) evening star; or literally, God-like star. The French Protestants were called HUGUENOTS. The origin of the word has greatly puzzled writers. Its etymology is only to be found in the Cymbrian or Welsh language. It is probable that the prominent reformer or founder of the Gallic Protestants was a Cymbrian Gaul; if so, his name was appropriate, for a more noble sect never existed. The Edict of toleration was proclaimed at Nantz, in 1598, under Henry IV; and after being in force 87 years was revoked by Louis XIV., in 1685, and the Huguenots in vast numbers expatriated themselves and sought refuge in Holland, England, Switzerland, and America. They preferred freedom of conscience in strange and distant lands to all the endearments of their ancestral homes beneath the bigoted rule of tyranny.
Hue, from *Hu*.
Jean, *for* John.
Jacques, *for* James.
Ion, source of being.
Llamai, steps, strides.
Lamanai, *a Brittany name.*
Llalu, to alternate, vary.
Llaru, from *lleru*, sharp, cunning.
Llenu, to veil, to envelope (*a Gascony name.*)
Louis or Luys, *same as* Lewis.
Legare, from *gar*, a limb or shaft, and French *le*, the.
Mathïeu, from Mathews.
Maurice, Morris.
Maury or Moray, from Maurice.
Mora, motion of the sea.
Moreau, from *mor*, sea, and *aw*, water.
Mol, congelation.
Molainu, to praise, to adore.
Moran, *contraction of* Morgan; also means a large sea-fish.
Morbihan, little sea.
Morben, a promontory.
Morlas, a sea, green color.
Manygault, from *man*, space, *ny*, universal, and *gault*, energy, power.
Malu, to reduce, to grind.
Melin, a mill.
Mordai, sea-shore.
Maul, *same as Scotch.*
Moise, from *moi*, to cast, to produce.
Noe, a shallow vessel, a dish, a tray

Nye, *same as Scotch and Welsh etymology.*
Negus, strait, narrow.
Plasu, extended area, large building.
Pra, to spread out.
Prau, from *praw*, a trial, a proof.
Pri, origin, a cause.
Prud, from *prud*, set time, a season; hence Prudhomme, a timely man.
Plas, an area, an edifice; hence La Plas, the place.
Robert, from Robert.
Ricard or Ricardo, from Richard.
Rowlan or Rowland, *same as Welsh etymology.*
Rollin, from Rholyn.
Ser, stars.
Sulé or Sully, from *su*, to extend round, and *lli*, a stream.
Segru, to separate, a secret.
Segur, composed, at leisure.
Seguryn, an idler.
Seron, a system of stars.
Sue, from *su*, that tends to pervade, a buzz.
Sori, to press upon.
Suryn, acidity.
Sur or Cir, state or quality.
Talma, from *tal*, towering, tall front, and *ma*, space or place.
Tirion, pleasing, pleasant.
Tobyn, a summit.
Tor, a prominence, a pinnacle
Tyrol, from *tyrawl*, heaped up, accumulated.

The etymology of a great many other Gallic names might be given, for which we have not space.

Among the men of note supplied by Brittany in France have been :—

Chateaubriand, and Abbe De Lammennais, both of whom were natives of St. Malo, Brittany.
Caillaud, the Egyptian traveler.
Constable Du Guesclin, *equivalent in his day to Marshal.*
Count Dara, author of the History of Venice.
Duguay Trouin, the naval hero.
Emile Souvestre, author of a work called *Brittany and the Bretons.*
Fouche, Minister of Police.
Laennec, the physician and author of the stethoscope.
Madame Savigne.
M. de Bourdonnaye.
Maupertius, Savary.
Mar'l Vauban, Bronssais, the physician and author of a new system in Medicine.

See HUGO's *France Pictoresque;* also, *Guide du Voyage en France.*

HOLLANDIC AND GERMAN NAMES OF CYMBRIAN ETYMOLOGY.

The existence of these names in Holland and Belgium and along the Elbe and Rhine in Germany, may be accounted for partly from the fact, that the aborigines of those countries were Cymbrian tribes, who were probably subsequently subdued, or forced to migrate farther west, by the Teutonic and other northern tribes—offshoots or descendants of the western Goths, themselves of remote Scythian origin.

A considerable number of the aborigines, like the Wends and other tribes, would remain and intermingle with the invaders and retain their aboriginal names, more or less corrupted. Holland had these names multiplied by the emigration of the French Huguenots, who sought refuge in that country.

Such names have in many cases received the prefixes of *Van*, as Van Allen, the son of Allen; and also the terminations of *man*, *land*, *wing*, *ving*, *or ing*.

Amar, excitement, a noise on all sides.

Astur or Astor, from *astyr*, regularity, a plain or uniform surface.

Alten, from *al* and *ten*; hence Altenburg.

Bog, a swelling, a rising up, [*also Scotch*]

Buren, *same as Gallic for* Buron; hence, Van Buren.

Bul or Bol; hence, Bolman, from *Byl*, a trunk or box.

Clin or Cline, to sparkle, a spark; hence, *Clin*-ton.

Cosyn, a single cheese.

Cot, a crop.

Dan, attractive, a fine object; *Dan*-ton [*also Gallic*]

DeLavan, from *lla*, expansion that is light or clear, and *fan* [pronounced *van*], a covering, a surface.

Duer, from *Duw*, God, and *er*, impulse.

Elbe or Alba, a high state of being. Applied to a stream it means that it has its source in high lands or mountains; hence, a high island might be called Elbe or Alba.

Eng, space.

Erbyn, to blunt, to allay, to soothe.

Francis, *same as in Welsh.*

Folk or Foulke, *same as Welsh*

Got, that which stimulates or drives out

Heber, Huber, or Hobar [hence Hobar] *same as in Welsh, Scotch, and Gallic.*

Hardi or Hardy, from *hardd*, towering, graceful, neat; [*also Belgic, Scotch, and Gallic*]

Hud or Hod, *primitive of* Hud-*son*, the son of Hud or Hod; or *Hod*-son, from *hud*, allurement, to persuade, etc.

Hog, *same as Scotch.*

Hogi, to sharpen, to whet.

Holl or Hull, hence Hollman, from *holl*, the whole, complete [Holland, the whole land.]

Hains or Hayne, from *hain*, to pervade, to spread, to influence.

Halle, from Hall, (*same as Scotch*) an old town of Wendish origin in Hanover, Germany.

Hoff or Huff, hence Hoffman, from *hoff*, loved, dear, beloved, lovely.

Holbar, omnific, causing all things.

Hotan or Hutan, *same as the Gallic.*

Kant, from *cant*, periphery of a circle, series of numbers, an hundred.

Kip, from *cip* (pronounced *kip*) a sudden effort.
Kis, from *cis*, a blow, slap, or sudden attack.
Kist, from *cist*, a chest.
Kissane, from *cis* and *an*.
Kissam, from *cis* and *am*, around.
Lop, buskins, a boot.
Ludwig, *synonimous with* Lewis *or* Louis.
Manny, from *man*, space, and *ny*, universal.
Ogden, from *og*, motion, expansive life, youth, and *din*, to surround.
Over, hence *Over*-man, from *ofer* (pronounced *over*) vain, prodigal.
Ollwell, all-seeing, power of foresight, seeing all things.
Ol or Ul, hence *Ul*-man, from *ol*, a mark, or a place.
Post, a projection, that which projects.
Postyn, a little post.
Pryne or Pryn, from *pryn*, to purchase, a merit.
Rhan or Rhand, hence Van Rhan [*the primitive of* Van Rensselaer] from *rhan*, a portion, a part, a share, a division.
Rhine, from *rhin*, that which runs through a deep channel between high lands, to carry off the lesser waters; the etymology of the river Rhine.
Ruggles, from *rugl*, quickness, fluent, free.
Sach, a small bag or pouch.
Sill, hence *Sill*-man, from *sill*, a component part.
Trave or Travis, from *traf*, a strain, a commotion or stir. Lubec in N. Germany is on the River Trave, and was anciently called Trave, having ancient Cimbrica Chersonesus to the north of it.
Vyse, from Wyse [*same as Welsh*]
Winans, from *win*, white, and *an*, an element.
Wit, from *wyt*, art; hence, De *Wit* which, in Cymbrian Gallic, signifies of wit, or of art.

ADDITIONAL NAMES.

Cochrane, from *coch*, red, and *rhan*, a division or mark.
Laurens or Lawrence, from *llaw*, hand, and *rhan*, a portion or division [*Welsh or Gallic.*]

Historical evidence exist in favor of the belief, that Bohemia and Moravia, as well as Lusatia, in Germany, were first inhabited by Cymbrian tribes; and, that the eminently missionary Protestant sect, known as Moravians, was founded by men of Cymbrian origin or descent. They were first heard of in 1170, at Fulneck, in Moravia, and hence their name.

At an early period they met with severe persecution, when a portion of them joined the Waldenses, in Piedmont, a Protestant sect founded about 1160.

Christian David, a missionary of their Church, carried their religion from Bohemia to Herrnhut, in Upper Lusatia.

At a later period Nicholas Lewis, well known as Count

Zinzendorf, became a convert and missionary of the sect, and was the first who established the Church in the United States, at Bethlehem, in Pennsylvania. Soon after Luther turned Reformer, the leaders of the sect in Germany held interviews with him, and acquainted him with their doctrines, which he approved.

It is also said, that the Methodist ceremony of *Love Feast* was adopted by the Rev. John Wesley from this sect; and also the custom of assigning separate seats to the sexes during public worship.—*See* BUCK'S *Theological Dictionary*; also, CRANT'S *Ancient and Modern History of the Church of the United Brethren*, 1780.

There is also reason to believe that the Magyars or Mygars of Hungary are the descendants of a Cymbrian tribe, known to the Greeks and Romans as *Pannonians*, from *pannon*, a Welsh word, which signifies "that which comprehends universality—an epithet for the Deity, the originator, the creator." The kingdom of Hungary rose in the 11th century, and the sovereign power was vested in Arfrad, a chief of the Magyar race.* It became powerful as a kingdom, and the bravery of the Magyars largely contributed to save Europe from conquest by the Turks.

We may note as a subject of interest that Wales, at this time, has several able Protestant missionaries laboring among their ancient fellow-countrymen of Brittany, though not without meeting with some persecution. They have distributed translations of the New Testament and many other religious books among them.

So large a territory did Brittany at one time occupy in France, that a writer of history has declared that the French empire was rescued from destruction by the indomitable courage of the Bretons; whose nationality became united to that of France by the marriage of Ann, Duchess of Brittany and daughter of Francis II., Duke of Brittany, with Charles, and afterwards with Louis XII., King of France.

The Bretons defeated the Huns, in a great battle fought near Nantz, in 445; and also aided in the defeat of Attila, near Chalons, as previously stated, thus powerfully contributing to save France from Scythian conquest and plunder.—See *Histoire Des Peuples Bretons Dans La Gaul et Dans Les Isle Britaniques, par Aurelien De Courson.* Paris, 1846.

The name of *Arfra*, or *Arfrad*, a Magyar, and first king of Hungary, corresponds with the Cymbrian etymology of *Ar*, faculty of speaking, and *Ffra*, prompt, ready, fluent, articulate clear, eloquent,—or an eloquent man.

ADDENDA.

HAVING omitted to insert notices of the following persons in a more appropriate place, we give them below.

GRIFFITH DAVIES, F.R.S., died in London, in March, 1855. He commenced life as a poor Welsh boy, and was self-educated. He did not learn to speak English until he was over twenty-one years of age. He wrote a Key to Bonnycastle's Trigonometry, and translated Newton's Principia into Welsh, which, however, with the exception of portions of it, was left in unpublished manuscript. His first publication was a work on "Life Contingencies."

He was the mathematical tutor of Sir John Franklin, and instructed him in navigation. He was employed at times both by the Bank of England and the Hon. East India Company in many labored computations.

He was elected a member of nearly all the leading learned societies of Europe, and was an ardent member of the Society of Antiquarians. At the time of his decease he was Actuary of the "Guardian Assurance Company" and "Reversionary Interest Society."

MILNE EDWARDS, the late distinguished physiologist, of Paris, was a native of Wales, and went to France when young.

His labored and ingenious experiments, with the philosophical deductions derived from them in support of correct physiological theories, won for him permanent and wide-spread fame in the scientific world.

THOMAS CHARLES, A.M., was born at Carmarthen, S. W. He was the founder of Sunday Schools in Wales, during their first establishment by Robert Raikes, in England.

He was one of the founders of the British and Foreign Bible Society, and was also author of a large theological dictionary, in Welsh, and several other standard works; some of which have been translated into English.

EDMUND PRYS, Arch-deacon of Merionethshire, in the reign of Elizabeth, was remarkable for his learning; and, among his other works, was his translation of the Psalms of David from the original Hebrew into Welsh verse, which is said to excel in force and beauty similar English translations.

We are limited in space, otherwise the list of Welshmen

whose names, both among the dead and the living, made illustrious in the walks of science, art, and literature, might be greatly extended.

Before closing, we may be permitted to allude to two or three persons of note, among many others who are still in the field of action.

The first is the present Chancellor of the Exchequer, in England, the Right Hon. Sir GEORGE CORNWALL LEWIS, Bart., M. P.

His family belonged to Radnorshire, Wales. His father, Sir Thomas F. Lewis, occupied a distinguished position as a public man; and represented Radnorshire in Parliament, a constituency held at the present time by the Chancellor, his son.

The family has been considered liberal and eminently practical in its political views. Sir George is the author of several able works, among the last of which was one entitled "On the Use and Abuse of Political Terms," which is said to be remarkable for its originality, practical applicability to ordinary political conversation and discussion, and "that no political student should be without it." He also at one time occupied the editorial chair of JEFFRY, and conducted with credit and ability the *Edinburgh Review*.—See the London *Illustrated News* of May 5th, 1855.

Another living individual to whom we have referred is Professor CHARLES DAVIES, whose modesty is only equalled by his worth, and whose pardon we must crave for introducing his name; which, however, we feel authorised to do, because we had the statement from his own lips, that he belonged to a Welsh family.

Mr. Davies for 20 years filled with great usefulness the Professorship of Mathematics in the U. S. Military Academy, at West Point. He is the author of 15 volumes of works on mathematical subjects, all of which, except two, are used as text books at the Academy, these two being supplied by other authors. Many of his works are extensively used as text-books in various academies and colleges of the United States.

Though less known to the world as an author, yet highly distinguished as a man of uncommon learning and research, and eminent as a divine, tempered with unusual modesty, we cannot close without referring to the Rev. WILLIAM R. WILLIAMS, the Pastor of the Baptist church, in Amity Street, New York.

His father was also a clergyman of great usefulness, and was a native of Wales; from whence he emigrated to New York, where he became pastor of the Oliver St. Baptist church.

Dr. Griffith, of Philadelphia, an eminent Physician, and one of the founders of the noble charity, known as the Pennsylvanian Hospital, was of a Welsh family.

Mrs. Dewitt Clinton, who died at Poughkeepsie, New York, July, 1855, was the widow of the late Gov. Dewitt Clinton, one of the greatest, and purest of men in the annals of the State. She was the daughter of Dr. Thomas Jones, the son of a Welsh Physician, whose father settled at Jamaica, Long Island, and was widely known as Dr. John Jones. He was attached to the Revolutionary Army as a Surgeon, and was a personal friend of Washington and Franklin. He was one of the founders of the New York Hospital, and a professor in the medical faculty, in Columbia College, at its first institution. He was the first successful Lithotomist in the country. Mrs. Clinton was his grand-daughter, having Dr. Thomas Jones for her father, and a daughter of Phillip Livingston, signer of the Declaration of Independence, for her mother. Maturin Livingston, a son of Phillip, married a daughter of Genl. Morgan Lewis.

Mrs. Clinton was in every sense a remarkable woman ; not less for her strength of mind, than for her noble good breeding, purity, and polish of manners. She was liberal and frank, and fully appreciated the great mind of her noble husband, and, the harder the storms of personal and political strife blew upon him, the closer her affections twined around him, while she nobly and devoutly cherished his memory to the last.

THE CYMRY AMONG THE PILGRIM FATHERS.

We may here incidentally state what we should have done at an earlier stage of our work: that among the Puritan Pilgrims who came over in the *Mayflower*, were several persons of Welsh origin or descent. And among whom was Capt. JONES, the commander of the *Mayflower*; and in the list of passengers were THOMAS ROGERS, STEPHEN HOPKINS, JOHN ALDEN, and JOHN HOWLAND, the latter of Gov. Carver's family.

The Hon. MOSES H. GRINNELL and his brother HENRY GRINNELL, two noble and distinguished citizens of New York, have lineally descended on their mother's side from the above John Howland, who was of Welsh origin. REYNOLDS, who set out as Captain of the *Speedwell*, which had to put back, was also said to be of Welsh origin. We are happy to state in conclusion that JOSEPH COGGSWELL, Esq., the worthy and learned librarian of the Astor Library, New York, is of Welsh descent by the female line, having sprung from the Phillips and Paysons of Ipswich, Massachussetts.

CONCLUSION.

The Cymbrian etymology of Hollandic, Germanic, and Belgic words, could have been greatly extended, but our space compelled us to be brief.

We know that our definitions may not accord with preconceived opinions, or in all cases prove rigidly accurate.

The subject was comparatively new to us, and surrounded with many difficulties. Being a native of the United States (but of Welsh descent on the side of both parents), we could not be expected to obtain that familiar mastery over the Cymbrian or Welsh language with the facility of a native of Wales.

Some persons may fancy that they can find in other modern languages, or in Latin or Greek the origin of many words which we have defined by their Cymbrian etymology. It must be remembered, however, that many Latin and Greek terms and words that occur in other languages are occasionally synonimous with those in Welsh.

The difference between the few Latin words found mixed in with the Welsh, and those used by the Romans, arises from the fact, that the former are uniformly derivative or radical, while the latter are most commonly quite arbitrary; which has led to the belief that these words came with the Cymbrian races, from their eastern origin, and existed anterior to the foundation of Rome.

Leaving the ingenious, if disposed, to seek in other tongues the definition of names differing from the etymology we have given, we can only say, that we have faithfully endeavored to give their actual and literal meaning in the Welsh. Many words of this language like the English have several significations for each; and also many of the words of the same orthography, varied only by the accent, have different or synonimous meanings with others differently spelled.

Local habits and customs, with the admixture of other tongues (especially on the continent of Europe) with the primitive Cymbrian language, has tended more or less to change its orthography and pronunciation.

All we have been able to hope for, has been, to approximate as nearly as possible, etymological correctness.

We trust that we have produced sufficient evidence to show the general analogy which exist between the Cymbrian races, and the etymology of their nomenclature.

The subject is interesting, and deserves the close study of those in search of correct ethnological history. We have pursued our brief and cursory investigations amidst daily interruption from other pursuits.

We consider that no man can properly investigate the ethnology of Europe, or the etymology of its Geography, or of the names of its inhabitants, unless he first makes himself acquainted, to a greater or less extent, with the Cymbrian dialects, corrupted though they may be, in different localities—the purest, oldest, and most unmixed specimen of which, extant, is that found in the Ancient Briton or Welsh of the Principality of Wales.

It may in conclusion be remarked, that the Cymbrian races of the west of Europe, and their descendants at this day, are found in the very van of modern progress and civilization in all parts of the world.

HISTORICAL SKETCH

OF

The St. David's Benevolent Society.

OF THE CITIES OF NEW YORK AND BROOKLYN.

[SUPPLIED BY A MEMBER.]

THE Semi-Centennial Report of the Ancient Britons' Benefit Society states that, about the year 1801, "The Welsh members of the late 'Albion Benevolent Society' formed another, designated the 'St. David's Benevolent Society';" which, like the "Albion," was of short duration. Its members after its dissolution re-organized themselves into an association for mutual aid, and keeping up "St. David's Day," under the title of "The Ancient Britons' Benefit Society." This occurred in the year 1805. It proved highly successful and, as will be seen by reference to a statement of its present condition, is now flourishing.

It is necessary to an understanding of the reasons of the failures and the success of these societies, to allude to the principal circumstances which produced them. The early Welsh emigrants who settled in this city were animated by sentiments of patriotism, benevolence, and self-protection. Benevolence being uppermost, they were naturally moved to organize themselves into a benevolent association. Their habits, industry, and savings, however, rendered such an association almost needless, except for an occasional outpouring of the nation's *amor patriæ* which animated them. To this end they celebrated St. David's Day—a day hallowed among the Welsh for its religious, benevolent, and patriotic recollections.

This day was usually devoted to the settlement of the accounts of members of the Benefit societies, when the country or non-resident ones attended. Their business being transacted, they would retire to some public house or hotel and pass the evening in feasting and social enjoyment—rehearsing in speech, sentiment, and song, interspersed with music of the harp, the valorous deeds of Cambria's ancient warriors—the picturesque beauty of her blooming dales and romantic hills—or, the no less inspiring theme of her fair and lovely daughters

From the simple and unpretending festival, conducted without reference to show or public fame, which marked the early celebration of "St. David's Day," it grew into a fixed and permanent institution; and the celebration of "St. David's Day" is now considered indispensable among the Welsh of New York, it being honored by the presence of many distinguished personages; among whom may be named, as standing guests, the Mayor of the City; the Presidents of the St. George, St. Andrews, Friendly Sons of St. Patrick, St. Nicholas, New England and German Societies, etc.

These annual oblations being performed and the attendant excitements allayed, the mind naturally, in a cooler but more practical manner, sought a more tangible and effective mode of displaying its true admiration for benevolence. In this state the contingencies of the future presented themselves to practical common sense. Hence a system of mutual protection presented itself strongly to the support of those possessing the true feelings of independence. The early Welsh settlers, though seemingly indifferent to the support of a purely benevolent organization, yet felt that they would promote the ends of charity among their countrymen more by the formation of a benefit society, for mutual protection against want, than by establishing a remedial society, to alleviate distress which might have been avoided. This plan of mutual protection has excited a beneficial influence. The Ancient Britons' Benefit Society has been established just fifty years. Its members at present number 174, and its funds on hand amount to $2,581 54. The monthly contributions of a member are twenty-five cents; his benefits in case of sickness are $4 per week; formerly the sum was $3. The Society has paid, since its organization, $13,569 20, for sickness and funerals, and $1,882 12, for expenses.

Its members are mostly practical mechanics and workingmen. A striking instance of the value of benefit associations is found in the following:—A member of the Ancient Britons' Benefit Society was afflicted with a stroke of the palsy, which disabled him for life; since his affliction, some twelve years, the Society has paid him weekly benefits to the amount of $1872, and which he will be entitled to receive for the balance of his days. Had this man been friendless and poor he would have become a tax upon the public treasury; no matter what might have been his vocation or his position in society previous to his affliction. He may have served his country and his race; brightened the pages of literature; delved in the laboratories of science; sung the praises of the brave, the beautiful, and the good, in the gifted strains of poetry—yet his sorrows would, perhaps, have only been deepened by the galling reflection that those upon whom he had conferred blessings and happiness, while he enjoyed the vigor of health and the means of self-support, were among the first to forget and desert him.

The penalties of improvidence may seem harsh and severe —can we say they are unjust? Nature provides man with the means of supporting and guarding himself through life; if we do not avail ourselves of the *means* she gives us, should we complain?

We remember of no instance when a member of either of the benefit societies has ever applied for public or outside assistance (except from his relations or immediate friends, and then not from absolute compulsion), that is, during his membership. The subject of life and health insurance, and mutual benefit societies, as a conservative means of strengthening the independence of society, demands the investigation of our legislators, and should receive their liberal support.

A Welsh beggar or pauper is, if not a phenomenon, certainly (without speaking egotistically of the race) not a common occurrence. May not their benefit or provident societies have had something to do in producing this result?

In commending benefit societies thus especially we would not be understood as detracting from the true merits of the subject of *Charity*. Charity is an attribute in our character of which we need feel no alarm in being over-stocked, or in its too free exercise towards our fellow-men. Our aim is to awaken the mind to a clearer comprehension of its meaning, and to the effect produced upon the general condition of society, by holding out inducements to men, in looking to public institutions for support in cases of misfortune and poverty, (which the cultivation and growth of public and private charitable institutions inclines them to do), instead of cultivating and fostering the principle of mutual support in the accumulation of a general fund, by mutual weekly or monthly contributions from their earnings, from which to draw in the event of sickness, infirmity, or old age. This is a duty we owe to ourselves and to society. For however charitable we may be disposed to our neighbour, and however cheerfully we may dispense our charities, that neighbour has no moral or just right to neglect providing for himself and his family in the time of his prosperity, and looking to us for support in times of adversity. Charity compels us to see that he does not starve or suffer; while his neglect, however, is nothing less than a crime and an imposition upon society.

With a view of diffusing our ideas upon this subject, we have thought that these remarks might tend to some good, and not prove inappropriate to a brief historical sketch of the St David's Benevolent Society. We may remark that in the various Welsh settlements in the United States it has been customary for the early settlers to organize some sort of society for mutual assistance and support. In some places where the settlers were mostly of the same religious persuasion, such assistance or support would be afforded by religious societies or the Church, but in larger settlements they would organize benevolent or benefit societies. Thus, in Philadelphia, in the year 1800, an association denominated "The Welsh Society of Philadelphia" was organized, and exists to this day as one of the noblest ornaments of that city; it having a large permanent fund and extensive cemetery grounds. As this is probably the oldest Welsh society in this country, we insert the following extract from its Charter and By-laws :—

"It is an opinion hardly to be controverted, that the inhabitants of this country are, in a social manner, bound to respect the virtue of hospitality to the stranger and the unfortunate. Whilst familiar circumstances seem to indicate this important truth, it must strike the intelligent mind as no less worthy of observation than of gratitude, that, when Divine Goodness imposed upon man a duty so essential to his nature and happiness, it was to be accompanied with a pleasure and satisfaction in the exercise thereof, which loses not its reward even in this life. On the contrary, "I WAS A STRANGER, AND YE TOOK ME NOT IN," is an address that few minds can contemplate without emotions of horror, and which even the misanthrope will rather deprecate than envy.

"Although the wretched of no clime or condition should be excluded from our aid and commiseration, yet we hold the maxim to be both just and natural, that those of the country and people of our ancestors have claims of far greater sensibility and of stronger obligation than others.

"Under the influence of those sentiments and impressions, the sons of St. DAVID, in the city of Philadelphia and its vicinity, have long since instituted a society for the humane and benevolent purposes of dispensing advice and assistance to Welshmen in distress.

"This ancient institution, so much the pride and honor of its founders and supporters, and so much the object of grateful remembrance by the many who have shared in its bounty and assistance, having been accommodated to existing circumstances from time to time, with respect to form, is now established by an Act of incorporation, and presented to the Society in the plan of the following Constitution.—

"ARTICLE I.

"For the purpose of more effectually affording advice and assistance to Emigrants from Wales, the following named persons, viz. :—Samuel Meredith, Clement Biddle, Morgan J. Rhees, Benjamin R. Morgan, Robert Wharton, Jacob Morgan,

Benjamin Morgan, William Jones, Richard Price, Jonathan Jones, Thomas Cumpston, Samuel Clark, Samuel Price, George Thompson, Michael Roberts, Robert Jones, John Davis, Richard Morris, Cadwallader Evans, jun., Owen Foulke, Caleb Foulke, jun., John M. Price, Joseph Price, Lewis Walker, Peter Evans, Joseph Roberts, John Evans, Edward Thompson, Richard C. Jones, William Lewis, Joseph Simmons, Joshua Humphreys, John Morgan, John Thomas, Samuel Miles, jun., John Wharton, James Read, John Cadwallader, Josiah Roberts, Griffith Evans, Franklin Wharton, David Ellis, James Ralph, William Ogden, William Nichols, Samuel Jones, Samuel Miles, Edward Jones, Israel Jones, Robert Morris, Enoch Thompson, Cadwallader Evans, Edward Tilghman, Richard Peters, Peregrine Wharton, Edward Roberts, David Evans, jr, Joseph Strong, Samuel Wheeler, John J. Parry, Elijah Griffiths, John Bowen, Mathew Randall, James Smith, Samuel Wetherill, Joseph North, Chandler Price, Joseph Snowden, George Clymer, John Haines, William L. Maddock, Isaac H. Jackson, William Smith, Thomas Wharton, jun., Jonathan Walker, Thomas C. James, Richard H. Morris, Paschal Hollingsworth, Richard Edwards, John Palmer, Owen Jones, Isaac Jones, John Owen, William Jones, Charlton Yeatman, William Preston, John Read, jun., John Jones, John Lewis, John Philips, Benjamin Jones, James Cruikshank, Benjamin Price, William Read, William Meredith, Joseph S. Lewis, Clement Humphreys, Samuel Parish, Thomas B. Zantzinger, Thomas Jones, Samuel Humphreys, Edward Edwards, Joseph Ball, Thomas Humphreys, Jonathan Smith, Pearson Hunt, Thomas Cadwallader, Joseph Higbee, Wilson Hunt, James Hamilton, William Hamilton, David Edwards, Ezekiel E. Maddock, Joshua Edwards, Joseph P. Norris, Thomas Parke, Gideon H. Wells, James Gibson, Benjamin Chew, jun., Robert Thomas, Richard Peters, jun., Abiah Brown, John Clifton, Daniel Smith, Thomas Allibone, Isaac Wayne, Charles Cadwallader, Henry Jenkins, Isaac Jones, Thomas Biddle, being citizens of the Commonwealth of Pennsylvania, and such others as they shall hereafter associate with themselves, being citizens of the said Commonwealth, are hereby erected into a body politic and corporate, by the name, style, and title of "THE WELSH SOCIETY" and by the same name, style, and title, shall have perpetual succession, and may purchase, take, and hold, by gift, grant, demise, bargain and sale, devise and bequest, or by any other mode of lawful conveyance, any lands, tenements, goods or chattels, real, personal, or mixed estate, and the same or any part thereof, from time to time, may sell, alien, convey and dispose of and shall and may have a common seal, which they may alter and renew at their pleasure. *Provided always, nevertheless,* that the clear yearly value or income of the messuages, houses, lands, and tenements, rents, annuities, or other hereditaments and real estate of the said corporation, and the interest of the money by them lent, shall not exceed the sum of five hundred pounds.

"ARTICLE II.

"Any person known to be of Welsh descent and proposed as a candidate by a member shall be balloted for at the next meeting; and, provided the votes of two-thirds of the members present appear in the affirmative, shall be duly elected. Previous to the next meeting after the election of a member, he shall sign the Constitution, and pay into the hands of the Treasurer eight dollars, when he shall be entitled to receive a certificate of his admission, under the seal of the society, signed by the President and Treasurer, and attested by the Secretary. Honorary members, however, may be admitted without being subject to the aforesaid conditions."

The early Welsh settlers in New York, who organized a society in 1800, were not so successful as their brethren in Philadelphia. This probably arose from the Welsh in that city having been more numerous and wealthy than their brethren in New York; for it will be perceived by the Charter of their society that it provides only for the assistance of emigrants from Wales and not for its members. Be that as it may, in New York several attempts were made before a society was thoroughly established, and then on the benefit principle—that is, mutual insurance among the members against sickness and distress. This was not accomplished, however, until after the failure of an attempt to establish a benevolent institution similar to that of Philadelphia, under the title of "The St. David's Benevolent Society," as mentioned in the commencement of this sketch. At the dissolution of this society its funds were divided among its members, who organized "The Ancient Britons' Benefit Society," and transferred them to the latter. Thus, the "Ancient Britons' Benefit Society" became virtually the legatee of the funds and trusts of the early "St. David's Benevolent Society," and performed its functions in a private or collateral manner, until 1835, when the necessity of some distinctive organization for benevolent objects was made apparent, and resulted in the establishment of an institution on the 9th November, under the title of the "St. David's Benefit and Benevolent Society," with the following Board of Officers:—

Genl. MORGAN LEWIS, *President.*

THOMAS I. JONES, *1st Vice-President.*
EDGAR W. DAVIES, *2nd* "

G. W. Griffith, *Recording Secretary.*
William Miles, *Corresponding Secretary.*
Luke Davies, *Treasurer.*

DIRECTORS.

Evan Griffith,	John Jones,
John Jenkins,	Daniel Jones,
Thomas George, jun.,	John X. Jones,
David Roberts,	John Morgan,
Joseph Morgan,	R. J. Williams,
William Price,	Robert Roberts.

Thus, after a repose of some thirty years in the bosom of the "Ancient Britons' Benefit Society," the benevolent disposition of the people sought means of greater expansion and of a wider range of usefulness and, at the same time, stronger expression of their patriotic and kindred national feelings; yet, keeping in view the special care of their countrymen found in distress. A new society was formed intended to combine the mutual benefit and benevolent objects in one organization.

After three years' trial, it was found that the two features did not work together: it was then determined to separate the benevolent from the benefit, and organize a purely benevolent society; which, however, was not fully accomplished until January, 1841, when the present society was formed. The benefit branch still exists, and is known as the "St. David's Benefit Society." (*See* extract from its annual Report, March 1st, 1855.)

The members, however, differed in their views, and refused to act in concert. A separation took place, the advocates of the permanent fund system withdrawing and organizing themselves as a society under the title of "The Welsh Society." The members of both societies strove to outrival each other in deeds of benevolence and liberality. After a few years' contest, and just before the death of the late lamented David Cadwallader Colden, who had served as President of the society for a period of about nine years, commencing in 1841, a reconciliation took place between the contestants; and the members of "The Welsh Society," upon the admission of the leading points of their Constitution into that of "The St. David's" Constitution, merged their society into that of the latter.

The following quotation from the Preamble of the "Welsh Society" well expresses the views and sentiments of the members of both institutions. We may simply mention that the points of difference between them was in relation to the establishment of a permanent fund and affording relief to emigrants. Sober reflection convinced each party that it was policy to compromise these points, and unite; which was done.

"The lessons of experience derived from the establishment and operations of benevolent institutions among the emigrated inhabitants of different nations in this city show, beyond a question, that they are not only practicable but exceedingly beneficial, and are calculated to raise the standard of national reputation and excellence in the same proportion that they watch over the conduct and welfare of those allied to them by ties of consanguinity, and encourage in the way of rectitude their steps. A society purely benevolent, and carried on by men capable of the undertaking as to means, talents, correctness of judgment, and honesty of purpose, must inevitably act as a *preventive*, in many if not in most cases, to the existence of those scenes of wretchedness and misery which in a greater or less degree exist among the children of every nation. When such instances of affliction do occur, it becomes the privilege as well as the duty of such an institution to relieve them so far as its funds will allow—not with the cold and uninterested feelings of a stranger, but with the warmth and affection of a parent.

"This society has for its great and fundamental principle, the virtue under consideration—*Benevolence*. But Benevolence does not consist exclusively in the distribution of alms—this is but a small portion of its efficient efforts towards the amelioration of human wretchedness. And this society, although it will take due and anxious care to provide for means to relieve urgent necessities, will, through its members and other sources, endeavor to procure employment for their fellow-countrymen, so as to place them in positions to relieve their own wants. To any high-minded and properly ambitious man, capable of performing his ordinary avocation, the kindness would be far more acceptable than making him the recipient of unconditional alms. *The procurement of employment for our destitute fellow-countrymen is also one of the objects of this society.*

"The treatment of emigrants on their arrival in this port has recently arrested public attention, and in one or two cases has justly aroused popular indignation. The eyes of our criminal tribunals are at length opened to behold the enormity of frauds daily practiced upon this unsuspecting, and too often credulous, class of people; and, in some instances, the cause of the emigrant has been signally vindicated in the punishment of their robbers. At a late trial in one of the criminal courts of this city, a gentleman of known respectability and of unquestionable integrity, who possessed the means of arriving at his conclusions to a degree of certainty which figures alone will afford, testified under oath that, during the year ending in December, 1842, the sum of $80,000 had been robbed from emigrants in the manner above alluded to. This species of modern robbery, filching, by the basest and falsest representations, from the emigrant his little all, thereby throwing him and an unprotected family wholly upon the tender mercy of strangers, with whose language he is frequently totally unacquainted, has for a long time called aloud to the benevolent for redress. This society will, with proper and efficient aid here and across the ocean, (which has already in part been promised it) make a strong and, it is hoped, a successful effort in eradicating this evil from the items of our national grievances."

It will be seen that the present St. David's Benevolent Society took its root as far back as the year 1800. The Welsh people possess a patriotic affection for their native land and their race, and are animated by a sense of duty to respect and to care for their poor brethren in distress. Their natural pride of character and love of independence lead them to form providential habits. They prefer assistance from mutual benefit or provident societies to receiving aid from charitable or alms-giving institutions. Still, they do not lack true charitable feelings; but, nevertheless, are neither instinctively nor by conviction inclined to favor the growth of charitable establishments.

Among the leading members of this society at its formation was its first President, the late Major-General Morgan Lewis, son of Francis Lewis, who was a native of Wales, and a Signer of the Declaration of Independence.

The General had once been Governor of this State, and was allied by marriage to the distinguished and honored family of the Livingstons. His name and the pride he took in boasting of his Welsh blood, which he said had not been crossed on either side of his family, exercised a very wide and beneficial influence on the welfare of the society.

Next in prominence, and of more extended usefulness, was the late David Cadwallader Colden*, second President, and son of the mayor of the city of New York, of that name.

Mr. Colden's descent from an ancestry of high fame, combined with the reputation he had acquired among the leading philanthropists of this city; and his great abilities and extraordinary activity in all schemes of benevolence, were also highly

* The following was accidentally omitted from the body of the work:—

CADWALLADER COLDEN of New York, grand-father of the late David Cadwallader Colden, discovered the mode of Stereotyping, or taking *Casts* from Types. He sent a description of it to Dr. Franklin, in 1779, who was then in Paris. The latter communicated it to Didot, a famous printer, and to Herbau, who had been his assistant. The process of the latter is said to be precisely the same as that invented by Colden. The art was first introduced into New York in 1813.—J. W. FRANCIS. See *The World's Progress and Dictionary of Dates*, by G. P. PUTNAM, 1851: Article, *Stereotyping*.

EDWARD DAVY, of London, said to be of Welsh descent, invented the first Electrical Chemical Telegraph, for which he obtained a Patent in England, in 1838.—*See History of the Electric Telegraph*.—A. J.

beneficial to the success of the society, and aided materially in placing it upon a permanent footing of equality and usefulness, with the leading national benevolent institutions of the city of New York.

The Vice-President of the society, at the time Mr. Colden was President, was the late Hon. Henry P. Edwards, one of the Judges of the Superior Court, a personal friend of Mr. Colden, and a descendant of the eminent divine Jonathan Edwards; and who also, from his well known ability, contributed largely towards the prosperity of the institution.

Upon the death of Mr. Colden, Wm. Miles, Esq. was elected President, and continued in office two years, during which period his indefatigable exertions, as well as his own liberal donations, have aided to augment the funds of the society, thereby contributing to extend the sphere of its usefulness.

At the annual meeting in March, 1853, Mr. Peter Roberts (one of its most liberal members) was elected its fourth President, and held office one year; upon the expiration of which Wm. Miles, Esq., was re-elected, and still continues its President.

In connection with the foregoing names may be mentioned the following gentlemen whose labors in their various capacities of officers and members contributed largely to the present prosperity of the institution. Thomas Ingram Jones, though not of late years an active member, was one of the founders of the society, and for a period of fifteen years was an unceasing laborer in its cause and in every other patriotic movement of the Welsh in this city. With equal credit and praise may be mentioned the names of William J. Williams, John Evans, David Roberts, John Morgan, Griffith W. Griffith, Daniel L. Jones, the late Daniel D. Jones, David Jones, Thomas R. Jones, Rev. W. R. Williams, D. D., Rev. Wm. Rowlands, Evan Griffith, Hon. Henry E. Davies, Hon. R. H. Morris, late Mayor, Capt. John Owen Rhees, Thomas J. James, William Griffith, Wm. Williams, Robert Evans, Lewis T. Roberts, Thomas Price, James Jones, Wm. Roberts, Alexander Jones, John Griffith, Morgan Morgans, Sen., Hon. Morgan Morgans, Jun., W. H. Danna, George B. Williams, Wm. Lewis, Owen Humphreys, Rhees Lewis, Thomas Lewis, Owen Jones, W. Lloyd, Edw'd Dolson, H. N. Morgan, Edward Walker, Chas. T. Cromwell, the late Gideon Lee, Evan R. Bebb, John Jeremiah, Wm. Bowen, M. D., David Morgan, Geo. Morgan, John Jones, Isaac Davies, Thomas Williams, Thomas H. Williams, the late Chancellor Samuel Jones, etc.

In keeping with the foregoing, it is proper to acknowledge the aid the treasury of the "St. David's Society" has annually derived from another Welsh institution in New York known as the "Cambrian Association," an organization which has beer in operation for nine years, and is composed of the younger portion of the Welsh residents and descendants of Welsh, of this city; whose annual entertainment has been the means of contributing over twelve hundred dollars since its formation to the permanent and distributable funds of this society.

Nor are warm thanks less due to the energy and devotion of the fair daughters of Cambria who, in various ways, have nobly contributed to the success and prosperity of her cherished institutions.

During the past year or two the Society has had to deplore the loss by death of several distinguished and useful members; among whom were the Hon. Henry P. Edwards, Edwin Williams, Walter R. Jones, John Griffiths, Thomas Price, and Capt. Thomas Thomas.

In conclusion, we may incidentally state that there are four Welsh churches in New York, in which the services are conducted every Sabbath in the Welsh language. They consist of one Baptist, one Wesleyan or Methodist Episcopal, one Calvinistic Methodist, and one Congregational church. Connected with these churches are large and flourishing Sunday schools.

There is a Welsh Paper published weekly in New York, with over 5,000 subscribers. There are also four monthly Magazines published in the Welsh language, in the United States. One is issued from this city, two from towns in Oneida County, and another from Pottsville, Pa.

The following named gentlemen were elected officers of the Society, on the third Monday in March, 1855 :—

PRESIDENT, WILLIAM MILES.

1st Vice-President,	G. W. GRIFFITH,
2nd "	ROBERT EVANS.
Treasurer,	DAVID ROBERTS.
Record'g Secretary,	HENRY N. MORGAN.
Corresp. "	WM. B. JONES.
Physician,	WM. S. BOWEN, M. D.
Chaplain,	REV. BENJAMIN EVANS.
Counsel,	HENRY E. DAVIES.

COMMITTEE ON BENEVOLENCE.

WM. ROBERTS,	JOHN REES,
JAMES JONES,	THOS. H. WILLIAMS,

JOHN PHILLIPS.

STEWARDS.

THOS. M. JAMES,
JOHN EVANS,
THOS. LEWIS,
OWEN JONES,
DANIEL S. OWENS.

COMMITTEE ON FINANCE.

GEO. B. WILLIAMS,
WILLIAM LEWIS,
LEWIS T. ROBERTS.

COMMITTEE ON LITERATURE.

ALEXANDER JONES,
THOS. R. JONES.
WM. J. WILLIAMS,
HUMPH. LL. WILLIAMS.

The following statement is made from the last annual report of the Treasurer, David Roberts, Esq., and presented at the anniversary meeting in March, 1855.

The total amount in the permanent fund, as per last report, dated March 17, 1854, was .	$2,272 57
Received from all sources during the year, .	230 00
Amount of the permanent fund on hand drawing interest, ...	2,557 20
Total Cash in permanent and distributable funds,	2,596 22
To which add value of Lots in Cypress Hills Cemetery, ...	150 00
Silver Badge of the President; Society's Seal; Library, etc., ...	150 00
.	$2,896 22

This sketch may appropriately close with the following extract from the report of the Finance Committee:—

"The condition of the Society at present is such as to commend it to the vigilant care and lively solicitude of all the truly benevolent and patriotic of our fellow-countrymen. It has already effected much good in relieving the necessitous, and the pleasing prospect of greatly enlarging its usefulness in proportion to the increase of its means."

The following statement shows the condition of "The St. David's Benefit Society," an insurance association for the mutual protection of its members against sickness and burial expenses.

It was originally started with a view of carrying out charitable objects in connection with those of benefit, but, after a fair experiment it was deemed policy to separate and conduct them under distinct organizations. This explains the fact of two societies bearing the name of St. David.

AN ANALYSIS OF THE REPORT, WITH A STATEMENT OF THE PRESENT CONDITION OF THE ST. DAVID'S BENEFIT SOCIETY.

Bond and Mortgage,	$1,000 00	
" "	500 00	
Cash in Sixpenny Savings' Bank,	569 38	
" Treasurer's hands,	77 17	
		$2,146 55

Present number of resident members,	77	
" " non-resident,	26	
		103

Receipts from resident members for the year,	$311 07½	
Receipts from non-resident members for the year,	103 62½	
Interest on bond and mortgage,	95 00	
" deposit in bank,	18 21	
		$527 97

Paid resident members for sickness,	$40 00	
" " " funeral,	30 00	
" non-resident members, for sickness,	84 00	
" " " funeral,		
		$154 00

Average annual receipts from resident members,	$4 04
" payments to " for sickness,	52
Average receipts from non-resident members,	3 09
" payments to " " for sickness,	3 23
Total expenses for rent, salary, stationery, postage, etc.	52 01
Total paid for sickness and funerals,	154 00
" receipts, interest, dues, etc.,	527 97
" payments, expenses, and benefits,	206 01
" amount of funds, March 1, 1854,	1,824 59
" " " " 1855,	2,146 55
Gain for the year ending March 1, 1855,	321 96
" " " " 1854.	276 32

Number of members	added for the year,	. . .	26
"	" died,	. . .	1
"	" expelled and withdrawn,	. .	0
"	" candidates forfeited,	. .	2

Accepted and approved, March 1, 1855.

WILLIAM MILES, *President.*

W. J. Williams, *Secretary.*

Mr. Thomas R. Jones was elected President of this Society, at the last annual meeting, March 1.

We will conclude this sketch with the following statistical table, exhibiting the number of associations and publications existing among the Welsh of the city of New York at this date :—

1 Benevolent Society—The St. David's Benevolent Society ; amount of funds, . $2,896 22

2 Benefit Societies—The Ancient Britons' Benefit Society and the St. David's.

4 Christian Churches, where the services are performed in Welsh language—1 Calvinistic Methodist, 1 Wesleyan, 1 Baptist, and 1 Congregational.

1 Welsh Military company—The Cambrian Musketeers.

1 Social Association—The Cambrian Association.

2 Welsh Newspapers—The Drych a'r Gwyliedydd and the Cymro Americaidd.

1 Welsh Magazine.*

The publication of this sketch of the St. David's Benevolent Society, with the accompanying Address, etc., has been made with the view of aiding the Treasury of the Society, from any net receipts that might arise from its sale.

The work can be had from the publishers, or may be ordered at the "Drych a'r Gwyliedydd" Office, 158 Chatham Street. By remitting the price of the book it will be forwarded by mail, and the postage prepaid.

* In reference to the present state of Welsh Literature, it may be stated that there are 13 Quarterly reviews and monthly periedicals published in Wales, besides six newspapers, all in the Welsh language.

Omission on Page 20 of the Address.

The Rev. Morgan Edwards, of a Welsh family, served as Chaplain in Washington's Army, during a good part of the American Revolution.

Note to Page 41 of the Appendix.

Ireland was conquered by Milesian Princes from Spain who established a kingdom there 1070 years B.C., under Heremon. His successors, it was said, introduced the Carthagino-Phœnician letters into Ireland, about 500 years B.C.

The country became divided, in the twelfth century, into five separate kingdoms, known as Ulster, Leinster, Meath, Connaught and Munster, besides a number of smaller principalities, which often warred with each other.

It is believed that the Milesians could not have been a primitive Cymbrian race, because that part of Spain from whence they came, possesses no Druidical remains, or other proof of a pre-existing Druidism. Neither were the Phœnicians or Carthaginians believers in Druidism, from whom their letters were derived.

The strongest proof of the primitive character of the Cymbri, was their Druidical religion, which radically distinguished them from the Goths and Teutons of the North, as well as from their extreme Southern neighbors.

It is true, that Druidism did at a remote period, exist in Ireland, and especially in the North, but it is contended that it was first planted there by branches of the Cymbri, anterior to the Milesian invasion, under whose sway, it gradually diminished, and finally disappeared after the introduction of Christianity.—See *The World's Progress, or Dictionary of Dates*, by G. P. Putnam; article "Ireland," with its Chronology, &c.

Note to Page 47 of the Appendix.

It is a curious historical fact, that the first *Christian* Prince or King in Europe was Lucius, known as King of Britain, A. D. 167. He was a native Briton, named *Lles ab Coel*, and called by the Welsh *Lleurug* and *Lleufer Mawr*, "*the Great Luminary*," and was said by the Welsh Triads to have been the great grandson of Caractacus Also, the first Christian Emperor, Constantine, called "the Great," was born in, or near York. His father, Constantius, died in York, England, July 25th, A.D. 306, and was succeeded by his son, who commenced his reign at York, in the same year.—*See* Thackeray, Vol. I.

Note to Page 65 of the Appendix.

We have mentioned, that the old Welsh name for London, and which is still retained in the Welsh language, was *Llun-*

dain, or *Thlyndain*, pronounced *Klundain*. It was Latinized into *Lundinum*, and Anglicised into Lundon, or London. The Cymbrian or Welsh etymology of London, therefore, is from *Llyn*, a pool or lake, and *Dain* or *Tain*, for Thames, (the sound of *d* being like that of *t*,) hence, a *pool* or *lake* on the *Thames*. It is supposed that the low flat, on the east side of London, known as the "Isle of Dogs,"—now a part of the main land—was at one time flooded by the Thames, and especially at high tides, and hence the name of *Llundain*, or *Thames Lake* or *pool*. We have said, that Liverpool came from *Flowing Pool*, that is, the tide flowed in and out of it. It is said that a pool once existed, where the Custom-house now stands, and that Castle Street, which leads to it, was once called Pool Street.

Avon (or *Afon*) is the generic name in Welsh for river, hence, *Avon Stratford*, *Avon Conwy*, *Avon Clyde* (or *Kluid*), in North Wales, and in Scotland; *Avon Derwent*, or Derwent water, from *derwen*, an oak (from whence was derived *Derwydd*, or Druid.) Hence *Avon Derwent*, means Oak River; *Avon Ouse*, from *wys*, pronounced ooys, water, and Avon Humber, from *hymyr*, meaning a short sea river. Hence, also, Cymbrian or Cumbrian mountains; Cumberland, from Cymbri-land, and Northumberland, from North-Cymbri-land. The River *Tay*, (anciently *Tave*) comes from *Taf*, pronounced Tav, to spread, to expand. *Aber* is the mouth of a river, Anglicised into *harbor;* hence, the great variety of names, in Wales, England and Scotland, which commence with Aber: such as Aber-Conwy, Aberystwyth, and Abermarlais, in Wales; and Aberdeen, Abroath, &c., in Scotland. Indeed, there is scarcely a river, mountain, or lake, of note, in England or Scotland, the etymology of which is not found in the Welsh (ancient British) language to the present day.

Note to Gallic Names, Page 109 of the Appendix

The etymology of Shakespeare's NAME, has greatly puzzled writers, and, to this day, no generally received definition has been given. We would, therefore, with all due deference, suggest that the origin of his name was Gallic, and probably derived from *Jacques Pierre* (James Peter), *Pierre* being sounded in French similar to *Peare*, in English; hence transformed by Saxon pronunciation into *Shacks*, or *Shakes-peare*.

In plain English, his name would then be *William James-peter*. The Saxons and Germans usually sound the J as S; hence, for Jacques they would say *Shakes*, for Jack (abbreviation of John) *Shack*, for Jones *Shones*, &c.

The supposition of its Gallic origin, is strengthened, from the known custom, prevalent in Gal and Britain, subsequent to the introduction of Christianity, of converting Scriptural names into surnames.

www.ingramcontent.com/pod-product-compliance
Ingram Content Group UK Ltd.
Pitfield, Milton Keynes, MK11 3LW, UK
UKHW021053270726
13967UKWH00012B/645